WHAT PEOPLE ARE SAYING ABOUT *BE MORE*

"*Be More* embodies my belief in servant leadership. It provides practical, strategic lessons that can help empower people to unleash their fullest potential and create the careers they crave. When employees understand their own strengths and values, and have the courage to voice their dreams, then leaders can provide guidance and growth opportunities that help turn those dreams into reality – and everybody wins."

Denise Morrison, President & CEO
Campbell Soup Company

"*Be More* is a catalyst for learning more about yourself and helping you develop a plan and vision to live the life you want to live. It's a must read for anyone thinking about what's next."

Shawn Parr, The Guvner & CEO Bulldog Drummond
Practicing Uncommon Sense

"I had a high school teacher in San Francisco who told me to become a journalist. So that's what I did. Crazy simple. But for those not so lucky, or those itching for a second career or purpose in life, Todd Putman's *Be More* is a godsend. As he writes in this most powerful guide you'll ever read: Time to unclip. Reach. And find the story you're born to tell."

Michael Moss, *New York Times* best-selling author
and Pulitzer Prize-winning journalist

"I read *Be More* at a crossroads in my life. By most accounts I was a success. But I was suffering terribly inside and I couldn't figure out why. *Be More* turned the lights on. My problem was that I hadn't taken the time to answer the fundamental question, "What do I want to be when I grow up?" *Be More* guides you through a series of revealing questions that cut to the core of who you are. In that truth is the juice, the power that unlocks everything. *Be More* is as much a transformative business book as it is a spiritual journey toward the fulfillment and joy we all seek out of life."

Lucas Donat, CEO, tinyREBELLION

"At Bolthouse Farms, Todd and I have experienced firsthand the impact that an authentic company mission can have for employees, consumers, and customers. It unlocks tremendous value for all stakeholders. In *Be More*, Todd shares the insights he learned from creating a company's purpose and creates a model that enables individuals to define their own mission to drive personal and professional success. *Be More* brings unvarnished truth with a sense of humor and allows Todd to connect with readers who desire more control over their careers."

Jeff Dunn, President, Campbell Fresh

"Some people still believe there's a methodical path to success that can be followed. *Be More* blows that path to hell and will set you on a much more fulfilling course."

John Palumbo, Founder of BigHeads Network

"Too often, people struggle because they don't know what they really want. Todd Putman has helped us all with this wonderfully readable book on how to know yourself, learn what you want, and then launch yourself in the right direction."

Tom Farley, Executive Director, The Public Good Projects

"A sprightly read on finding a career that aligns your skills, values, and passions."

Adam Grant, Wharton professor and
New York Times bestselling author of *Give and Take*

"Whether it be an entrepreneur pitching me an investment, anyone trying to figure out their career direction, an artist trying to break through, or a student wondering what or where they should study, I ask all to give me the same two things. First, "Tell me what you are dreaming about doing" and then, "Tell me the story of how you get there." Seldom is anyone prepared for both. Ironically, we can tell the stories of others way better than we can tell our own. Maybe it is time to put down the biographies and start finding our own story and this is just what *Be More* helps us do. If you don't think you have a story, then think again and plunge yourself into this book. When you finish, you will be ready to take control of where you want to go and even more, have others want to help your story end just the way you have always dreamed."

Rusty Rueff
The Kennedy Center President's Advisory Committee for the Arts
Chairman Emeritus The GRAMMY Foundation; Board Member Glassdoor

"Those lucky enough to count Todd Putman as a manager, colleague, or friend are well aware of Todd's passion for helping those in his closest circle find a career path that fuels their passion and allows them to achieve their full potential. By authoring *Be More*, Todd has made it possible for anyone to access the thinking and tools he's used to guide countless people through this process. Don't expect to read it and be done, this involves some hard work and deep introspection, but if you see the process through, you'll have a clear set of criteria to help you find out how you can *Be More*."

Doug Worple, Founder and Chairman of
Barefoot Proximity, a BBDO company

"Todd Putman is, without a doubt, one of our world's greatest marketing minds. *Be More* reveals the secrets to his success, but, more importantly, it shows all of us how we can find that success in our own lives. It's a must read for anyone early in their career trying to find their way, and it's a good reminder for the rest of us that there's always room for more. I highly recommend *Be More* for anyone looking to find greater fulfillment in their professional life."

John Hoffman, Executive Vice President
Documentaries and Specials, Discovery Channel

Be More

Be MORE

FIND YOUR TRUTH, TELL YOUR STORY, & GET WHAT YOU WANT OUT OF LIFE.

by TODD PUTMAN

with LORI SPARGER

Future Pull Group, Inc.

FUTURE PULL GROUP, Inc.

BE MORE:
Find Your Truth, Tell Your Story, & Get What You Want Out of Life
Todd Putman with Lori Sparger
Copyright ©2015 by Todd Putman
All Rights Reserved

Cover and Interior Design: April Bobeck

Published in the United States of America by Future Pull Group, Inc.
First Printing October 2015
978-0-9962776-1-7
First Edition

To the loves of my life
—Rachel, Bailey, and Noah—
I couldn't possibly ask for more.

—T.P.

For my dad,
my first, best editor.

—L.S.

TABLE OF CONTENTS

Foreword by Sam Kass I

Introduction.. VII

1 Project You.. 1

2 Have We Lost Ourselves? 17

3 Nobody Cares 29

4 Goals.. 41

5 Skills.. 57

6 Values.. 71

7 Passion 83

8 Reality Check.. 95

9 Adding It Up.. 107

10 Applying SVP.. 121

11 Everything Changes 133

12 What's Next?.. 143

Acknowledgments 151

Author's Note.. 155

The Authors.. 157

Notes.. 161

FOREWORD

It was an honor when Todd asked me to write the foreword to *Be More*. From our first meeting at the White House, when I spoke with him and Bolthouse Farms CEO Jeff Dunn about leveraging the power of marketing for healthier eating, Todd and I have always connected. We share a mutual understanding, a dedication to what we want to accomplish and how we are going to go about it. We also share a passionate commitment that grounds us both and directs what we do.

On the surface, our belief in helping people eat better, in promoting healthier eating, unites us. But as I learned more about the book and what Todd wanted to achieve with *Be More*, I realized that it runs deeper than that. At the end of the day, whether it's about making healthier food choices or empowering people to fulfill their potential—or as the book says to *Be More*—it's all about enabling people to live better lives. That's a pretty easy commitment to get behind, and it speaks to the kind of person I know he is.

Our conversation about the book came just as I was leaving the White House and the *Let's Move!* organization. As is often the case, a life change prompts us to look back even as we move forward. For me, the years in the White House offered an amazing opportunity to participate in important policy initiatives and to help guide the national conversation about eating better and combating the rise in childhood obesity. As I look back, that was all fueled by a commitment to learning, to preparation, and to self-awareness. It came from a genuine interest in people and in the basic impact of my work. And when your work is food, that impact is fundamental.

It's easy to recognize the opportunity at hand when the president-elect invites you to come to the White House. The subtler opportunities are harder to recognize. But those are the moments that made all the difference. Those are the moments that brought the other things within reach. When you know who you are and what you want, they become much easier to see.

For me, those moments began when I was in college. I wanted to learn more about cooking, and I wanted to see the world. So I applied to a study abroad program in Vienna to finish my history degree. And I didn't get in. But I was determined, and eventually I managed to elbow my way into the program. Once I was there, I tapped my network and was able to meet the best sous chef in Vienna. The day he invited me into his kitchen was life-changing. I worked for free for about a year, just for room and board. Even as I learned about cooking, I began to think more about the broader goal of feeding people. I started thinking about the choices I made in the kitchen, and the impact of those choices on the food system. Every piece of that experience helped shape the person I am today.

I left the States driven by curiosity—which seems to me the most important word in the hard conversation about finding your passion. Be curious. Be open, learn, engage with smart people, and put yourself out there. It's critical. We don't all find our life's passion at the same age or in the same way, but when you're curious, and maybe a little bit fearless, you can find the thing that will light you up and change your life.

Too often, I think, people become focused on a job or a title, and not the kind of work they want to do or the kind of people they want to be. I never said, "I want to go work in the White House on food issues." What I did say was, "I love food and I want to cook and see the world." I didn't know what my career would ultimately look like, but I started thinking about the influence I wanted to have. I began working and studying food policy, and by the time I came back to Chicago from Europe, I had direction.

That's what makes *Be More* so resonant. It's a commitment to knowing who you are, what you're about, and what you want to accomplish in order to make a bigger difference in the world. As I look at my work with Todd to use food marketing to promote healthier eating, we're trying to do something new and to do something big. All of that is powered by passion.

As I stand at the crossroads between what I've done and what I have yet to do, I know that there's not a single moment that defines me. We are all the sum of our experiences. But when we embrace the message of *Be More*—and move through life with a greater understanding of what we're good at, what matters to us, and what we want to achieve—our ability to effect meaningful impact grows exponentially. And when more people are empowered to live life that way, the benefits will make all of our lives better. With *Be More*, Todd may have found his greatest opportunity for impact yet.

It's a privilege to introduce it.

SAM KASS | New York

What do you want to be when you grow up?

INTRODUCTION

"YOUR TIME IS LIMITED, SO DON'T WASTE IT LIVING SOMEONE
ELSE'S LIFE. DON'T BE TRAPPED BY DOGMA – WHICH IS LIVING
WITH THE RESULTS OF OTHER PEOPLE'S THINKING.
DON'T LET THE NOISE OF OTHERS' OPINIONS DROWN OUT
YOUR OWN INNER VOICE. AND MOST IMPORTANT, HAVE THE
COURAGE TO FOLLOW YOUR HEART AND INTUITION. THEY
SOMEHOW ALREADY KNOW WHAT YOU TRULY WANT TO BECOME.
EVERYTHING ELSE IS SECONDARY."

Steve Jobs, *Stanford University Commencement 2005*

It seems like it should be so easy. "What do you want to be when you grow up?" It's not a new question. In fact, people start asking us the question before we're even old enough to remember the first time we were asked. It's a completely straightforward question. There's no subtext or nuance. It's merely a question of where your heart and intuition might take you. And yet, over and over and over again, I have been blown away by the consistent inability of incredibly intelligent, successful, highly competent, and otherwise articulate individuals to respond to that simple question with anything beyond a frozen, blank stare, a rambling stream of unconnected gibberish, or even gut-wrenching tears.

Over the course of my career, many people have come to me for advice on their careers, for help in taking the next step. They know they want more—just more. So eventually, I come around to asking that question. And almost without fail, they can't come up with an answer. The inability of people to say what they want results in an appalling number of extremely capable people who are not fulfilling their potential either professionally or personally.

Looking back, I started using the question "What do you want to be when you grow up?" as a non-threatening way of moving forward a conversation about career. Somehow, though, it becomes overwhelming. But it shouldn't be. It's a question about what you want to do next. That's all. It's not irrevocably defining. It's a question for today about where you would like to be tomorrow and the day after. It's not about defining your life for the rest of your life. When you start to approach the question that way, it becomes much more accessible.

Beyond the inability to answer that question, there are many reasons people find themselves adrift in their careers. It is often easier to move forward without pausing for introspection. Life comes at us fast today with no sign that is likely to change. Being caught up in a swirl of responsibilities and commitments, being harnessed by technology that allows endless connectivity, can dull our sense of duty to ourselves. Yet it is critical to realize losing our center, our sense of self, jeopardizes not only our ability to communicate our unique value and the mission we hope to achieve in the world, but also our best chance for happiness.

Until we take time to look inside, to understand and to articulate what we are good at, what matters most to us, what passion inspires us, we cannot find our truth. We cannot advance our life's mission. We cannot reach toward more. Without that, we are merely walking shadows, buffeted through life at its whim, rather than creating the most fulfilling personal journeys that we can during our short walk on this planet. We will not be as productive as we might, and we will not be as happy as we might. And that seems to me to be a waste of this one life we are given.

I see a fair amount of pushback against what some people characterize as the frivolous idea of following your passion. It has been bashed as elitist and self-indulgent. At one level, I get that. I recognize that there absolutely are people out there for whom the idea of doing what they love in a job is far from their day-to-day to reality. But I also know that many people could be doing something they love as part of their reality, if they choose to make it happen. At the May 2014 Milken Institute Global Conference in Los Angeles, studio executive and movie producer Jeffrey Katzenberg silenced a room with the assertion that people should follow their skills, not their passion, to find success. To me, that leaves out way too much of the story.

Katzenberg's words refute the common refrain that following your passion is the path to happiness. And he's not wrong. It's not as easy as simply following your passion. But his conclusion, that you should follow your skills with the hope it might become your passion, is a bad answer. Skills, passion, sure those are key proof points to help chart your path to success. They simply aren't enough though. The truth of who you are may have no stronger measure than the things you value. Your values shape who you are and can guide your journey toward a fulfilling life. Until you incorporate a thoughtful awareness of your values into the equation, it will never add up.

It's not as easy as simply following your passion.

In my career as a brand manager and marketing officer, I have inspired some of the country's top companies to tell their stories as part of a comprehensive brand strategy. From the deeply analytical culture of Procter & Gamble to the emotional storytelling that characterizes Coca-Cola to the mission-centered rebirth of Bolthouse Farms, I have seen the profound impact that genuine self-awareness creates. In each of those companies, the process of understanding who we are, what we represent, what we want to accomplish, how we share that story for greatest impact, and both recognizing and embracing our corporate and brand personality, has broad application.

Over time, my conversations with friends and colleagues who needed, or were thrust into, changes they could not yet envision became more and more frequent, and almost stupefyingly similar. In response, I developed a simple exercise derived from the lessons of crafting brand strategy. I re-purposed those tactics to help people. Just as we do in the consumer product world, the Skills, Values, Passion (SVP) Exercise forces people to peel back the layers, to better understand themselves, to think about what they want to do, to recognize what they do well, to identify what matters most, and to write it all down.

Once you can better communicate your personal story, you'll be able to move your career and life forward. It's about your skills, yes, but it's also about your values and your passion. That trifecta combines to create a comprehensive picture that is both relevant and validating. The SVP Exercise, which enables you to identify those points, is the frame upon which this book is built.

Deeply understanding your skills, values, and passion is essential to telling your story in a powerful way. Being a great storyteller is about more than simply telling a story. It's about being compelling. It's about being inspirational. It's about having a hook that makes people want to listen from the beginning straight through to the end. It's about having heart. And conviction. And the courage to put yourself and what you believe in the world for others to see. Finding your truth is the first step in learning to say what you want. Because when you can tell your story, when you become the storyteller of your own life, people won't just hear you; people will listen. It's time to make people listen.

People, of course, are neither corporations nor are they products. That is what makes the SVP Exercise the most compelling and meaningful project of my career. More than simply establishing a personal brand, SVP layers in the human dimension, incorporating the elements that factor in to allow you to move purposefully forward equipped with an authentic story that illuminates your truth and communicates your mission.

You want more, and you need to learn how to say what that means.

Moving beyond just developing an understanding of your career interests and goals, SVP focuses on the whole person, taking into account the life you live as well as the job where you work. You want more, and you need to learn how to say what that means.

Make no mistake—this is an exercise. There is homework. This isn't an ethereal discussion of what you're good at and what matters to you. SVP is a purposeful and straightforward way of identifying your five skills, four values, one true passion—the ten points which will allow you to write your story. You won't be lost in the weeds trying to figure out how this works. We'll work through it together with practical direction for how to complete each step.

I am indebted to a group of friends and colleagues who have shared their insights after having completed the SVP Exercise. Their comments help illuminate the work and validate the very human reactions this process produces along the way. They add a depth and humanity to this book for which I am very grateful.

Over the course of writing *Be More*, we have engaged in interesting conversations about how you should approach this story. It's not a hefty book, and it's not a difficult read. You could easily finish it on an airplane flying across the country, and I suspect some readers will do that. But in a conversation near the end of the writing process, one of my Bolthouse Farms employees, Julie Soley, worked through the SVP Exercise using the book as her guide. Her comments on how she read it offer an approach that makes sense. It's an approach I hope you will consider.

"What I do is, I hide in my bedroom, I lock my door, and I just read," Julie says. "Sometimes I read a paragraph over and over or a chapter over and over. I just want it to stick. After I am done with my reading for the night, I actually get in my car and leave my house. I go for a ride, and I process everything that I've just read. I think about what it means to me. It just gives me time to process what I've read before I have to go back to being a mother and wife."

The thoughtfulness with which Julie approached the book, and the time and care that she spent thinking about its lessons and quietly thinking about her life, allowed her to move through the SVP Exercise in a seamless way. It may not be how you will read this book and tackle your homework, but it was effective for Julie.

It is unquestionably true that we routinely spend an amazing amount of time managing things, while we spend way too little time managing ourselves and charting our life's journey. But it is time that must be spent. Through the SVP Exercise, you will craft your personal story as an integral tool to aid in understanding and articulating the unique value you bring to the world and the mission you want to advance in a way that is both authentic and relatable. Equipped with that narrative, you can focus on how you will bring your story to life.

To be clear, this is not intended to be a guidebook to the corner office. It can be that for some readers, but the application of what this book teaches is broader than mere career advancement. By reaching inside to understand what makes your eyes light up and how that relates to your strengths and what truly matters to you, my intent is to enable you to maximize your potential—to be more.

As it evolved, I have used the SVP Exercise with hundreds of people over the past two decades and have had the notion of a book in my mind for quite some time. So why now?

That question has two answers.

First, I saw a pressing need for a practical, usable, accessible guide to lend some clarity to one of the fundamental questions faced by all of us throughout our lives: What do you want to be when you grow up?

Across the spectrum, no matter their age, people are looking for something more.

A 2014 Harris survey reports that only 14% of workers believe they have the perfect job, and more than half of workers surveyed want a different career. The vast majority say that they are not in the job they had anticipated. (Anticipated? The lack of intent in that, the passivity of it, is mind-boggling.) In 2012, a full issue of the *Harvard Business Review* was dedicated to the question of happiness. Over and over again, surveys of Millennials point to an interest in "meaningful" employment but a consistent difficulty in articulating what that means to them. Across the spectrum, no matter their age, people are looking for something more.

Second, I found a writing voice that allowed me to talk about one of the most important topics on the planet in a manner that I believed would make people listen. It was imperative to find a way to reach people that was colloquial and funny, smart and sophisticated, that juxtaposes a sensitive recognition of the fear engendered by the level of personal introspection this exercise demands with the clear-eyed ass-kicking that is sometimes needed to move people forward.

As with so many things in life, timing is everything. *Be More* comes at a time when it can address a compelling need. As the national conversation points to the demand for a more productive, adaptable workforce, this book aims to empower the untapped potential of an existing and incoming labor pool that will propel economic growth, ingenuity, prosperity, and, yes, happiness.

This book began without an agent and without a publisher. If you ask, some people will tell you that's not the way to begin such a project. But in the face of something that has lived in my mind and in my heart for so long, with an opportunity to finally tell this story, walking away was never an option. After completing a first draft, it seemed that the truest thing to do was to listen to the lessons of the book, to control its evolution, to put this story into the world ourselves. Self-publishing has been a learning experience at every turn, and absolutely the right decision to make. You see, I believe when you set a goal and find a special intersection of skills, values, and passion, there is no part of "it's hard" that merits giving up. That's when it's time to dig deeper and push harder. With this book, it was time to give voice to something I believe can touch people in the most meaningful way of all: One person at a time.

Now, it's time to help you say what you want, to craft the story that will empower you to *Be More*.

TODD PUTMAN

Project you

ASK YOURSELF THIS:

What are you good at?

What energizes you?

What do you contribute?

1
PROJECT YOU

"IN THE DEPTH OF WINTER I FINALLY LEARNED
THAT THERE WAS IN ME AN INVINCIBLE SUMMER."

Albert Camus, Author and Philosopher

Wherever I go, whoever I talk to, everywhere I look, I see people who want more out of life—more impact, more opportunity, more fit, more balance—just *more*. And more often than not, the longing for more is tied to career. But what that more should look like, where to find greater fulfillment, too often remains undefined. As a result, rather than moving forward with intent, many people fail to fulfill their potential, not because of lack of ability, means, or opportunity, but too often because so very few can even say what they want.

Some of the happiest, most successful people share one special quality. It's not a certain expertise, not a singular personality trait. Nope. The common thread is an uncommon, and very purposeful, alignment of their exceptional skills, the values that guide their actions, and their true passion. Early in my career, I started looking, really looking, at the successful people around me. I tried to understand what had made them that way. Often they were driven. Almost without fail, they were goal-oriented. But the really interesting thing they shared was an absolute love for what they were doing. I realized what I was seeing, time and again, were people with an abiding belief in their work and an extraordinary commitment to doing it at a high level. Sure, it was work. But they didn't act like it, and they didn't talk about it that way. In fact, when I talked to them, I found myself getting excited, too, because they were so into what they were doing.

What I was noticing was pretty simple really. These people who were extremely successful, these people I aspired to be at some level, had found a way to take what they did best and apply it to what they cared about. They had found a way to pour their hearts and their talents into what was most meaningful to them. As a recipe for success, an intersection of skills and passion seems like a no-brainer. It's not a new concept—we've all heard it. But as I looked more closely, I saw something more. Completing the picture was the harmony of their skills and passion aligning with their personal values. Taken together, skills, values, and passion create a balance and strength that empowers you to find your truth and to achieve more.

At some point, I realized the most important thing: Success is not some special space reserved for a select few. Anyone with self-awareness and commitment can aim for that target, for their own intersection. It's not particularly hard to align your skills, values, and passion. We all

Taken together, skills, values, and passion create a balance and strength that empowers you to find your truth and to achieve more.

have the ability to enable our capacity to advance our personal mission, if we can take the time to listen, and to really hear, what's in our brains, our hearts, our souls. The fact is, I believe that for many of us, what we love is what we could be doing every day—if we had the clarity to recognize it and the imagination to envision it. But for too many of us, seeing where that is in our lives, let alone getting there, is another story. It is, however, a story you can learn to tell.

WHAT DO YOU WANT TO BE WHEN YOU GROW UP?

To tell that story, your story, you need to recognize and communicate your unique value. You will learn to see what makes you different, better, special. I assure you, each of us truly is. Ultimately, you need to be able to answer one simple question. What do you want to be when you grow up? The words are ones we've heard for as long as we can remember, but don't take them lightly. For many people, that's a remarkably difficult question. Saying what they want to be, what they want to accomplish with their lives, exactly what getting more out of life means to them is not always an easy thing. But it's an incredibly important thing. In fact, I believe it's pretty much *the* thing.

The question should not be paralyzing. It's a question of what you want next. And perhaps most importantly, it's not a question you will only answer once. It's a question you will answer over and over and over again throughout the course of

Your life can be bigger, bolder, more fulfilling, and it's completely in your hands to make that happen.

your life. Your answer will change, and that's great. What you want to be when you grow up should be a moving target. As you meet goals, as your priorities change, your perception of that question and how to answer it will change as well.

There's no doubt that getting to that answer requires considerable effort. As I talked with more and more people over the years who were unable to say what it was they wanted, I developed an uncomplicated way to help them identify the qualities that lead to an understanding of what makes each of us unique. With the Skills, Values, Passion (SVP) Exercise that represents the homework of *Be More*, you will work toward defining yourself in a straightforward manner. By identifying your exceptional skills, your core values, and your true passion, you develop the self-awareness to answer the question of what you want to be.

Your life can be bigger, bolder, more fulfilling, and it's completely in your hands to make that happen.

Yes, *your* hands. But that's not half as scary as you think it is. In fact, there are way scarier things than that. Consider this. To make it happen, you have to ask yourself, "Who am I?"

Let that sink in for a minute.

Who am I?

This isn't about the easy stuff. Sister. Brother. Teacher. Runner. Oh those certainly are elements of who you are, but to get to the good stuff, you need to move beyond the labels and the checkboxes and look for what's real, to take control of your life and your story so you don't let someone else take it from you.

THE SVP EXERCISE.

With the SVP Exercise, you will work toward those answers in a methodical, purposeful way. By identifying your five exceptional skills, four core values, and your one true passion, you gather the insights to answer the question: What do you want to be when you grow up?

It's not the exercise that's difficult here. Once you reach below the surface and genuinely express what makes you distinctively you, you'll see the puzzle come together with surprising ease. And be assured, we each have some mixture of qualities that makes us unique and valued in some way, even though we often fail to see it in ourselves. In fact, the

Some of the most capable people on the planet suffer from a failure of vision, of courage, of determination.

The SVP exercise

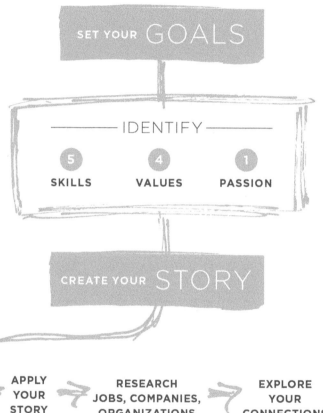

SET YOUR GOALS

——— IDENTIFY ———

5 SKILLS   4 VALUES   1 PASSION

CREATE YOUR STORY

APPLY YOUR STORY RESEARCH JOBS, COMPANIES, ORGANIZATIONS → EXPLORE YOUR CONNECTIONS

ENGAGE YOUR NETWORK TO REACH TOWARD YOUR GOALS

failure of so many people to see that—to celebrate it, to pursue the bold future that is within their ability to grasp—is the very inspiration for this book. Some of the most capable people on the planet suffer from a failure of vision, of courage, of determination. This results in a colossal waste of potential: potential for good, for innovation, for change, for happiness. To me, that feels unacceptable.

Life is not about finding yourself. There is not some preordained destiny into which you will stumble, at least not one that looks like anything but a stumble. Life is about creating yourself. It's about knowing who you are, what you want, and how you will get it. To answer those questions, to envision your boldest future, to empower your life's mission requires the clarity, commitment, and courage to pursue it. You only get one life. Don't you want to own it? Let me put it this way: Don't wait to get pushed off a cliff—swan dive.

Remember, the SVP Exercise is designed to help you know yourself in a way that allows you to find the intersection of your skills, values, and passion, to get you to that sweet spot where what you do best and what you care about most converge. It's about taking a hard look at your whole life at work and at home. Careers don't live in a vacuum. They are part of our lives, and our lives are complex with a lot of moving pieces. When you can say how all of those pieces can function best for you, your work will be more fulfilling and you'll be able to maximize the specific combination of qualities that only you bring to the table.

> Careers don't live in a vacuum. They are part of our lives, and our lives are complex with a lot of moving pieces.

Add a dash of luck, the right connection made at the right time, and more will be within reach. Perhaps even more importantly, the confidence and self-esteem that result from knowing that you are being true to yourself will bring a special sense of peace and happiness as you recognize that you are controlling your life and claiming your place in the world. I have seen the look in people's eyes when this happens. It's a powerful and profound moment when people begin to move forward—in control—in a way that they have defined.

MEANINGFUL WORK. AND THAT WOULD BE?

There's a great deal of research out there right now on Millennials. It's a demographic that pollsters, retailers, and others want to understand better, for lots of reasons. But I believe much of what studies have learned about Millennials is true for people of all ages. Studies of Millennials show a great priority placed upon meaningful work. In fact, the 2015 Deloitte Millennial Survey found that a "sense of purpose" is why 60 percent of those surveyed chose to work for their current employer. That number increases to 77 percent among super-connected Millennials, those who are more active social network users. Two years earlier, the same survey showed that the majority of American Millennials believe the primary purpose of business is to improve society. Noteworthy among the many mentions of the importance of meaningful employment, whether among Millennials or workers of other demographics, is the lack of a concrete definition of what makes work meaningful.

When you think about it though, that's really unsurprising. A blanket definition of "meaningful work" defies logic. What might qualify as a meaningful job to me may differ widely from what it means to you. What we deem meaningful is deeply personal, reflecting our individual goals, beliefs, and values. It takes a lot of self-reflection and a clear understanding of what matters to you most to tease out your own definition of meaningful work. This part of knowing yourself allows you to move forward in a way that balances your truth with your personal sense of mission.

We talked about labels earlier. Think about them and what they mean in your life. The labels rest on the surface, but they can be easy to hide beneath. Have you ever chased a job because the label appealed to you, perhaps even more than the job itself? Are there things you have never tried, jobs you have never pursued because a label said it wasn't for you? Have you missed out on challenging opportunities because a label held you back? Have you denied yourself the option of chasing your wildest imaginings because you were constrained by a label that said "Don't, it's not for people like you"? What sense does that make? "People like you"—are you really going to let someone limit you that way? Grab the label, and rip it off!

Now, it's gone. Feels better already, doesn't it? So ask yourself this: What are you good at? What energizes you? What do you contribute? What do you bring to the world? What motivates you? What makes you want to get out of bed in the morning and engrosses you so that you hate to go to bed at night? (A little suggestion: Grab a notebook and a pen now. Things are going to start flying through your head, and you need to write them down. You'll come back to them later.)

All of these things are elements of who you are, and perhaps more importantly, who you can become. See, once we started talking, it got a little less scary, didn't it?

ASK YOURSELF THE TOUGH QUESTIONS.

There's a catch of course. There's always a catch, right? Alongside those questions, you also have to ask tough questions of yourself and those around you. What aren't you so good at? Are the things you most care about aligned well with your strengths? Too often, we don't ask the tough questions for which we don't want to hear the answers. But you need to ask them.

My long-time colleague Bill Levisay says, "It's always better to know." To know your strengths, to know your weaknesses, to know the areas in which you can apply yourself, learn, stretch, grow, and reach for new areas of strength is invaluable information. I have a profound admiration for Bill's ability to go deeper. His insistence on facing the tough questions and the tough answers head-on is exceptional. He helped me see that the apprehension tied to asking difficult questions is like going to the dentist. Once you've asked—once you've gone there—you realize it was never as bad as the oppressive expectation of how bad it might be. Not asking leaves you on a treadmill going nowhere.

Once you have the answers, once you really know the problems, you are positioned to work toward solutions. And that's always a better position to be in. Just ask. An honest answer never killed anyone.

Our objective is preparing you to answer in a very thoughtful and purposeful way this question: What do you want to be when you grow up? In one form or another, over time, many people will ask some version of that question. Where do you see yourself in five years? Same question.

> Once you have the answers, once you really know
> the problems, you are positioned to work toward solutions.

What do you want to accomplish? Yep, that's essentially it yet again. It's about you, just you, and moving toward an outcome that reflects your individual capabilities and opens the door for you to consciously recognize and pursue what you want. Acknowledge and embrace the fact that you absolutely bring something to the world that no one else does. Who else is informed by your particular array of experiences? Who has your specific collection of skills guided by your core values? Who brings to the table precisely what you do? No one, I promise you that. Know yourself, find your niche, and move forward faster.

EMPOWER YOURSELF MOVING FORWARD.

As you work through this book, I want you to feel empowered to move your life forward, to embrace the inspired future that we talked about, and to tell your story in a way that feels right. Otherwise, all that happens is you bought a book. And maybe read it. That works out pretty well for me, but it's really not the point. It's sure not why I spent the time creating this book. I didn't write it for me. What's in here has been part of my life for years. I wrote it for you.

As you work through the SVP Exercise of *Be More*, what you will find is a story—your story—that allows you to position yourself in terms of career and avocation. You will learn to say the things that you know are on your path to finding the fulfillment and happiness that moving forward with intent can bring. It's your story—to own and to tell. If you don't, someone else will. It happens every minute of every day. People size you up. They see you in a context that defines you. If you don't create that context, if you don't tell your story, someone else will. In that moment, you lose ownership of the story that's all about you. If you don't say what you want, people around you will assume you already have it or perhaps even worse, they will assume they know what you want and move you in a direction that isn't right for you. Unless they know what you want, they have no way to help you get it. That's why you have to be able to tell your story. Think of that story as your personal brand.

All right. Stop. No eye-rolls allowed. Marketing. Brands. These are not the devil. They aren't. It's all about storytelling. And the best storytelling, like the best marketing and the best brands, is memorable. It is concise. It's purposeful. It's evocative. It may be colorful. But most importantly, it's true, really true. One hallmark of a great brand is the uncompromising truth of the story it tells and its unquestionable alignment with all it represents. As the face you present to the world, your story is the single strongest element in the backpack you will carry on your path moving forward. There's no more powerful way to be remembered and to set yourself apart.

It's your story—to own and to tell. If you don't, someone else will.

BE REMEMBERED FOR THE STORY YOU TELL.

When you say what you feel, when you say who you are, it is an immense thing. In that moment, with those words, you define your place in the world. You stake your claim to what you want to accomplish, and you set your life's mission when you can find your truth and say who you are. It will guide the choices you should make, telling you when to say "Yes" and also when to say "No." And so the work that goes into it, the reflection that brings you to your story, should be deliberate, intense, thoughtful, sometimes painful, and extremely purposefully orchestrated. It may require the deepest dive into yourself you have ever taken. It is scary. I get the fear of uncovering and embracing your true self, but I've also learned that the fear ebbs as the empowerment of becoming exactly who you are overcomes it.

"The construct of coming at it with the simplicity of one passion, four values, and five skills, is very approachable but also profound," says Jack, a former colleague who spent an extraordinary amount of time and introspection as he completed the SVP Exercise. "It's simple, but it's profound. You can't articulate your passion without doing a lot of work." It *is* a lot of work—get ready.

> When you say what you feel, when you say who you are, it is an immense thing. In that moment, you define your place in the world.

A lot of work, yes, but the prospect for return on your investment of effort is undoubtedly worth it. In one of the most memorable character introductions in American literature, F. Scott Fitzgerald described Jay Gatsby's smile, saying, "It understood you just as far as you wanted to be understood, believed in you as you would like to believe in yourself, and assured you that it had precisely the impression of you that, at your best, you hoped to convey." That idealized description captures the opportunity that lies before you as you conceive your personal story. It is yours to write and yours to tell, honestly, but also exactly as you choose. It is the opportunity to define your relevance in the world and to create the impression of yourself that you would most like to convey and that will best help you achieve your goals.

EMBRACE YOUR UNIQUE DIFFERENCE.

Don't be afraid of where that story takes you. It's about truth—your truth. The things that make you interesting and special may feel untraditional and off-center. Embrace them. That is exactly where your uniqueness lives. Hold onto it with both hands. The things that made you different in high school may have made you an outlier. Those are the very same things that will elevate you above the masses in your life. Don't ever be afraid to be you. Be authentic. If you don't, your life will never resonate in a genuine way, and the story you tell won't point to what will make you happier.

There's another reason your story is so important. Once you develop it, once you can articulate it in a truthful way, it will empower you. Your number one goal is to tell your story better than anyone else, before anyone else, and in a way that's relevant, emotive, and memorable. The strength of your personal story can become a self-fulfilling prophecy. "How so?" you ask. "Just because I say it, are you telling me that it will come true?" There might be more to it than that. But know this: An aura of purposefulness can take you a long way in this world. Quite simply, if you look like you know where you are going, you will be amazed at the people who will let you—even help you—get there. Your confidence will inspire you, and it will inspire those around you.

If you look like you know where you are going, you will be amazed at the people who will let you—even help you—get there.

A number of years ago, the former head of Walt Disney Studios, founder of Disney Theatricals, and director Peter Schneider led a master class for graduate acting students at Purdue. The discussion turned to auditions. The students, mostly twentysomethings, talked about the stress and angst of a process that in their view was about a dissection of them in search of their weaknesses. Schneider, a guy with no soft edges, told them something fascinating. At an audition, he said, as the director, he roots for a great performance. His goal is to find someone exceptional to fill a role, to make a production great. Rather than looking for weaknesses, rather than trying to weed out, his objective is to find the person who makes his eyes light up. So, while the actors felt that auditions were about looking for the ways in which they did not measure up, the director brought a very different perspective to the table. Every time the door opens and a new person walks into the room, he told them, I am hoping, praying, that this will be the one. I am desperate for you to succeed.

It's time to create your story. People love a good story.

But mostly, they love happy endings.

IT'S YOUR STORY TO OWN AND TO TELL.

Explore Self.

Know Self.

Express Self.

have we lost ourselves?

WHAT ABOUT YOU:

What do you want?

Where are you going?

Who do you want to be?

2
HAVE WE LOST OURSELVES?

"MAYBE THE KNOWLEDGE IS TOO GREAT AND MAYBE MEN ARE
GROWING TOO SMALL. MAYBE, KNEELING DOWN TO ATOMS,
THEY'RE BECOMING ATOM-SIZED IN THEIR SOULS."

John Steinbeck, *East of Eden*

It's time to think about telling your story, but first, it helps to understand why that can be so difficult. Why is it so hard to say what you want to be when you grow up? Too few of us really listen to what's in our brains, in our hearts, in our souls. Too few of us take the time to understand what matters to us. Too few of us find the words and actually say what we want.

Think about this: When is the last time you allowed yourself to dream, to let your imagination take you for a ride? And let me be clear, this isn't about what happens on your pillow fast asleep. When is the last time you allowed yourself to simply think, in a quiet room, in the quiet of your mind? When is the last time you seriously thought about what you want to be when you grow up, who you want to be before your time is up?

Silence.

Does that mean you've already accomplished all that you want and that you've met all of your goals? You've lived a full, happy, productive, successful life, and your plan for the future is locked and loaded. Wait. No. Maybe not, not yet; you are reading this book, after all. In the back of your mind, there must be a thought you want something more.

Let me be clear. It is altogether possible that you are perfectly happy and you are personally and professionally fulfilled with a fully-developed plan for your future. If so, that's terrific, but then this process may not be for you. It's hard. It's messy. It's uncomfortable. It might well upset your applecart. If your applecart is already upright and rolling along exactly as you would like, that may not be an outcome you want. But again, you are here. I think that's because you want something more, something that right this minute, you can't even say out loud.

What about this? How many times did you post on Facebook today? How many tweets did you send? How many Instagram pictures did you share? That's a lot of you out there for all to see.

Or is it?

CAN YOU SAY WHAT MATTERS TO YOU MOST?

If tonight you had three hours to spend with your best friend in the world, talking about nothing but you—your hopes, your dreams, your aspirations—do you know what you would talk about? Remember, this is all about you. It's not about your kids or your family or your dog, just you. What do you want? Where are you going? Who do you want to be? Are you prepared to have that conversation? Can you articulate who you are? Have you thought about what you want? Have you written it down? Can you make three hours of meaningful conversation?

My best guess is no.

Of course, it's not as easy as simply saying what you want. You also need to recognize what matters in your life and how all of those pieces fit together. Serial entrepreneur and former Apple and Redbox executive Mark Achler is a firm believer in pursuing your passion and understanding what matters most to you. "Life is short. Work should be fun," he says. "It takes courage to take a risk and follow your dreams."

It's pretty hard to argue with that. Achler's early career was marked by both the courage to pursue a dream, and the courage to leave behind a job he loved for the wife he loved even more. In the early 1980s, a newly-married Achler moved to California to join Apple. His wife wasn't enamored with the idea of relocating to the West Coast. He promised her that if she wanted, they would return home to Chicago after a year.

Achler worked in Apple's inner circle, alongside Steve Jobs, and orchestrated the product launch of the Apple IIc in spring 1984. It was a heady time at the innovative company on the cusp of introducing its Macintosh computer. Nevertheless, when the year ran out, his wife still longed to return to Chicago and family. So they packed up, returned home, and left California and Apple behind. It's a decision Achler, who has followed his passion for innovation by starting four companies over the years, does not regret. He has found a balance of skills, values, and passion that has been both successful and fulfilling.

ARE YOU LOST IN THE FLOW OF INFORMATION?

Having a sense of yourself and what matters to you most in your life is irreplaceable. You have this one life, this one shot. You may win, you may not. Shouldn't it all be in pursuit of what matters to you? And yet, really knowing what that is seems strangely elusive. We get lost in the fray. We are peppered with information in today's world. Round the clock connectivity means we are always on. Phone, email, text messages, social media, the entire Internet—it's always at our fingertips. Failing to respond immediately is a purposeful decision. A missed call is an ignored call.

We are never alone. There is no quiet in our minds.

There's no "missing" a call any more. "I was outside. I didn't hear the phone." Bull. It's always in your pocket. And our expectation of others is exactly the same. One ring, then voice mail—they are on the phone. Two rings, then voice mail—call screen. It's no mystery, we all know it.

The flow of information coming at us is non-stop. New stories, new statuses, new posts, new tweets—they feed a ravenous need to be entertained, to be connected, to have our glass unendingly filled to overflowing. We are never alone. There is no quiet in our minds.

And apparently, a lot of people aren't terribly comfortable with the idea of quietly thinking. According to research by University of Virginia psychology professor Timothy Wilson, people would rather inflict pain on themselves in the form of a small electric shock than simply let their minds wander. No kidding. In his study, two-thirds of the men, and a quarter of the women opted for a shock from a 9-volt battery when tasked with simply thinking for 15 minutes. Ouch.

In the spring of 2014, I had the amazing opportunity to hike more than 100 miles along El Camino de Santiago in Spain with a group of friends. The number of incredible experiences connected to that trip would fill yet another book. But there was one thing I learned that really speaks to this issue. On the Camino, there is nothing but time—time for thinking, time for conversation. As we walked and talked, I was struck by the sheer depth of conversation that seemed reserved for the Camino.

It was while walking the Camino that I read the first draft of what is now *Be More*. Before that, it had been a bunch of chapters that were reviewed, discussed, dissected, connected, but they were only pieces. It was, as T.S. Eliot said, "a heap of broken images." One day, I walked with a woman from Romania, a woman walking not just a section of the Camino as I was, but the entire Way of St. James. At some point, I asked her to tell me her favorite part of her journey. Her response continues to resonate with me. She said simply, "I see the Camino as one big piece." I realized that was how I had come to see this project. I had stopped looking at it as chapters or words. I was thinking about the whole thing; I was seeing it as a book for the first time. I would read at night and then walk the next day and feel just effervescent, happy that this thing that had existed in my mind was at last coming into the world. Having the opportunity to see it first along the Camino gave me the peace to really see it—without distraction—with fresh, clear eyes. Since then, the book has changed in many ways, but that first understanding of what it would become holds a special significance to me.

IT'S TIME TO UNCLIP.

Too often, our conversations are clipped, cut to the bone in unceasing deference to our over-scheduled lives. Give me three bullet points, and let's move on. We're pressed for time, distracted, and along the way, we too easily settle for interactions, professionally and personally, that only tickle around the edges of who we are and how we feel. It shapes our relationships with others, and, I believe, our understanding of ourselves as well.

Comparing the Camino to my daily life, it's easy to see why, in the relentless company of an overwhelming flow of noise, we miss out on time for introspection, for self-reflection, for the simple act of being alone with our thoughts, and for the daunting task of engaging and truly knowing ourselves. Purdue English professor Margaret Rowe once pointed out, "You're going to live longer with yourself than anyone else, and you have to know how to use your imagination to make your life richer." In the words of Albert Einstein, "Imagination is more important than knowledge. For knowledge is limited, whereas imagination embraces the entire world." That brings me to the question: How well does your imagination serve you? Do you know how to use it to make your life richer?

So what, you ask? So I don't spend time alone, so I read a lot online, talk to people a lot. I don't just sit around and think. Who cares?

The fact is, you *should* care, because the danger is that you've lost yourself. Your sense of who you are, what you want, where you are going can easily get lost in the din of information that skitters across the surface of the water but never ventures below. Remember, you're the one who doesn't know what you'd tell your best friend about your biggest dreams and plans for your future.

IS THAT REALLY YOU ON SOCIAL MEDIA?

Think about your social media self. How many pictures have you posted of yourself? How many flippant statuses? How many inappropriate tweets? Google yourself and consider what comes up. Is that really the face you want to present to the world? To your future employers? To your grandma? What is it about social media that entices us to devote so many hours to it, to share so much of ourselves on it? A 2012 Boston University study on why people use Facebook cites two fundamental reasons: The need to belong and the need for self-presentation. No doubt about it, there's probably a lot of your self presented on Facebook, right? But how deliberate is that presentation?

We can share more of ourselves with the whole world than any generation before us. And yet what is the connection between that public persona and our personal truth? How much truth is there in the face you present to the world through social media? How much of what you think, what you feel, what you absolutely believe does it represent? How much of you, the real you, is reflected in the electronic face you present to the world via social media? Every day offers an opportunity to write a piece of your autobiography online. Take a minute to think about this. Is that really your story as you would choose to tell it?

During the 2014 holiday season, one of the "it" gifts was the selfie-stick. We can't get enough of selfies. What do your selfies say? Do they reach down to your heart, to your soul? Do they represent the best parts of you or are they careless pieces thrown into the roiling wave of the World Wide Web as though they were impulsive bits of ephemera washed up on the beach, gone again with the next high tide, and given barely a thought? (But you don't really think those things are gone, do you?) Are we so cavalier with our images and our random thoughts because we too rarely consider the next year, yet alone the next decade? Do we fail to recognize that how we represent ourselves in the world—even the cyber world—is unquestionably part

How much truth is there in the face you present to the world through social media?

of what defines us? It matters. Doing the same thing over and over and over again and being surprised that the outcome never changes makes no sense. But it seems to be a trap into which many people fall. To move forward, to bring more purpose to your life and your career, requires stepping outside your comfort zone, taking risks, and making yourself uncomfortable. If you want something different, you must be prepared to *do* something different. Life is not an endless well, even though we often live as if it were. Our time is finite. Why wait?

> If you want something different, you must be prepared to *do* something different.

THE TIME TO DO SOMETHING NEW IS NOW.

To fulfill your goals, to reach for more, is hard work. You have to earn it; it's not a trophy for participating on a T-ball team. And first, you have to know what you want.

When I was growing up, my grandfather was a huge influence in my life. Pops pushed me hard. He was a self-made man, an entrepreneur, a pragmatic risk-taker. He left home in Oklahoma as a teenager and made his way in the oil business, or as he called it, the contracting business. He came to Indiana where there was less oil but also less competition and created the life he wanted. He didn't aspire to be J. Paul Getty, but he was extremely successful. Working for him in the oil fields, I learned the importance of an honest day's work. Along with that, from the time I was little, he instilled in me the belief that I had a responsibility to succeed. In his view, and at some level by extension in mine, I could be president of the United States. Over the years, that's never been the goal on my horizon, but having goals and writing them down have been part of my life since I was young. For as long as I can remember, I've always had a clear idea of what I want and a detailed plan for how to get it.

As you tackle the work of understanding your truth, people who are important to you will be part of your conversation. You will need to ask them hard questions—uncomfortable questions—about where your strengths lie, what your weaknesses really are, what matters most to you in the world, who you are. People who lift you up, who see you with clear eyes, will enrich this process. There's a use for social media and technology. Don't hesitate to maximize the capabilities of our digital age to enhance your personal connections in this process. In fact, that can be an important part of how you take this journey. The depth of your connection isn't measured by the mode of communication you choose. It's about the honesty of your interactions. It's about your truth and your willingness—your courage—to share it with others.

> People who lift you up, who see you with clear eyes, will enrich this process.

STEP INTO "WIDE AWAKENESS"

The late Maxine Green, a noted professor of philosophy and education, was an advocate of the need for personal reflection. She coined the term "wide awakeness." In an interview on *Edutopia.org*, Green said, "The only way to really awaken to life, awaken to the possibilities, is to be self-aware…. Without the ability to think about yourself, to reflect on your life, there's really no awareness, no consciousness. Consciousness doesn't come automatically; it comes through being alive, awake, curious, and often furious."

Green's concept of wide awakeness is all about clarity, about being fully present in your life, about being totally awake and totally alive. It's no small task to spend the time to examine your life, but alongside the other things that fill your hours, few should be a higher priority. It's your life, and if it's not worth the time to you, if you don't want to commit to yourself, to lay it on the line for yourself, what does that say? Put another way, with four seconds left in the game, down by one point, winners want the ball.

It's your life, and it's time to call for the ball.

When you are pummeled by too much information, pushing it aside and peeling back the layers to know yourself requires a purposeful effort. If you were likely to stumble upon yourself, and who you might become in the fullest, most deliberate, most extraordinary articulation of yourself, you'd have done it by now. We all would. You won't turn a corner and magically bump into your destiny. It doesn't work that way. To envision your boldest future, to achieve more, requires the clarity, commitment, and courage to pursue it.

So how do you pull all of the pieces together, find the clarity to know what matters most to you, recognize where your greatest opportunity for impact and for happiness lie, and know what you want to be when you grow up? With the SVP Exercise, you will work toward the answer to the question in a very straightforward way. We'll walk through it step-by-step to enable you to cut through the noise and find the quiet to know your true self. By identifying your five exceptional skills, four core values, and your one true passion, you gather the data that underscores your personal story and empowers you to find your truth, work toward your mission, to reach for more.

> To envision your boldest future, to achieve more, requires the clarity, commitment, and courage to pursue it.

Your inspired future awaits.

WHERE IS THE CLARITY TO FIND WHAT MATTERS MOST TO YOU?

5 Exceptional Skills.

4 Core Values.

1 True Passion.

nobody cares

DO YOU HAVE THE COURAGE:

To truly identify your strengths?

To acknowledge your fears?

To give voice to your dreams?

3
NOBODY CARES

"IN THE DARK NIGHT OF THE SOUL,
IT'S ALWAYS 3 O'CLOCK IN THE MORNING."

F. Scott Fitzgerald, *The Crack Up*

You're excited. You're energized. You're ready to get started. You're looking ahead and thinking about how this plays out and who you can enlist on your team.

As you work through the process of teasing out the qualities that make you different, better, special, your family, close friends, and mentors will all play important roles in helping you move forward in an authentic way. Their input and insights will enrich the process of helping you recognize and define your strengths and what matters most to you. The truth is: You can't do it as well without them. But don't kid yourself, you are the captain of this team, and only you can move it forward.

Sure, people do love happy endings, but achieving the happy ending you really want, that's all up to you. When it comes right down to it, nobody cares that you get exactly what you want.

It's true. Nobody cares about your career, that you fulfill your potential personally and professionally, or whether you accomplish your life's mission. Nobody cares.

Stop looking at me like that. It's true.

"It's not true," you say, "not in my life. My spouse cares. My parents care. My friends care. They love me."

Sure, but who cares? We are talking about two entirely different things here.

Your spouse, your parents, your friends—there's no doubt they love you deeply. Of course they want you to be happy, and they want you to have a good life. They do care. But moment of truth—their investment in you has limits.

Now you've got that look on your face again. "How can that be?" you ask. "They love me." Of course they do.

And they may, in fact, be invested in your personal happiness. Your spouse will be happier at home if you are happier, and probably even take pleasure in being somehow responsible for your happiness. Your parents will be delighted when you land a job that renders you self-sufficient, although your personal fulfillment may be of less interest to them. Paying your own cell phone bill, I promise you, they'll love that. Your friends will be ever-so-much happier if every lunch with you does not devolve into a bitch session, because eventually, that gets really old.

> But don't kid yourself, you are the captain of this team, and only you can move it forward.

I DON'T CARE. YOU DON'T CARE.

What you need to realize is that loving you and being personally responsible for your career and your happiness don't live on the same continuum. Do you remember the last time you offered to help a friend, to make an introduction, to lend a hand? What was your time commitment there? Half a day? An hour? Five minutes on an email? Of course, your offer to help was heartfelt and genuine, but you have a life of your own, your own responsibilities, your own obligations, your own mortgage to pay. Really, how much time are you going to spend on someone else getting their shit together? They told you what they needed. You sent the email, and you moved on. How much time did you spend trying to decide if that was the right thing for them? How much time did you spend thinking about whether that path was their best career move? How much time did you spend considering whether this was the thing that would bring your friend happiness? Not a lot. Maybe none at all. You didn't care. You were doing what they asked, checking a box, crossing an item off your To Do list. And then, you let your friend's next call go to voice mail, because really, you were done.

Make no mistake: Eventually, yours will be the call that goes to voice mail, and no one will call you back. Face it. And when that moment happens, it hurts—a lot.

Only weeks after 9/11, I was fired as vice president of marketing at Princess Cruises. I didn't see it coming even as I walked into the room, and my boss led off the conversation with a comment about what a big thinker I was. In the end, the significant—and more personal—shock was the lack of support as I suddenly faced the prospect of a job search I didn't expect. I was floored by the calls that weren't returned, by how shallow the pool of help turned out to be. At first, I was devastated that help didn't materialize. But eventually, after a lot of tears and finally coming to grips with that cold, hard reality, I was empowered by the fact that it was all up to me. I didn't need to wait for anyone, I didn't need to rely on anyone. What happened next in my career was all mine. I owned it. And ultimately, I was energized by that reality. You need to embrace that truth as well.

Nobody cares as much as you *should.*

Recognizing that nobody cares is not pleasant. I'm not saying it's easy to accept that realization, but it's important. Nobody cares as much as you *should*. To see that and move forward empowers you to pursue your own destiny. Nobody cares isn't a statement about the people around you. It's about you. It's about your responsibility for articulating and pursuing the career you want. To expect someone else to manage your life, to give away your responsibility for your personal fulfillment, makes no sense. Whose investment in you, in your happiness, in your success matters more than your own? Who can truly say what will make you happy? It's up to you to know it, to say it, to move toward it. If you aren't helping yourself, why would someone else want to help you?

What's that sound? Sounds like the deafening silence of realization. Of course it's you. It was always you. So you can sit in a corner and cry, or you can be liberated by being in charge. (Like I said, I tried the crying thing. It didn't get me very far.) You don't have to rely on someone else. You are in control. What could be better than that?

A colleague from my days at Coca-Cola in Atlanta, Jeff Crow, says he chuckled when I shared the outline for this book with him, and a draft of this chapter. "So few people realize that nobody cares," he says, "but it's so true. It's your career, and you have to manage it yourself." It's rare for anyone to spend a career with a single employer, so it's important to be able to pack up, go to the next place, and manage that transition. I've seen what happens to people who don't do that. Someone else will manage it, and that's not someone who cares about enhancing your career and supporting your vision of what matters in your life.

You are in control. What could be better than that?

YOUR EMPLOYER DOESN'T CARE MOST OF ALL.

And let me be perfectly clear. While the fact that nobody cares is true regarding the individuals in your life, the truth of that statement in terms of your employer is staggering. Yes, it's true that companies invest in their employees. They will train you, mentor you, and nurture your talents. But when you are no longer relevant to the broader goals of the organization, your talents, and most definitely your personal goals, will be of no consequence whatsoever when the time for downsizing or reorganization arrives.

I learned that lesson early in my career at Procter & Gamble. During a pretty unfiltered late Friday afternoon conversation on a company plane, I responded to a question from CEO John Pepper about ways we could do things better at P&G. I guess he called my bluff, because soon after I was asked to join a group tasked with strengthening our global effectiveness. About thirty of us spent six months in a basement where our team developed more than 180 recommendations for corporate restructuring. That kind of rebel thinking invigorated me. The notion of reconstructing the company was pretty cool. In that dark, spartan basement, outfitted with metal desks and no hint of personality, we turned a cold eye to the organization to re-envision how we should move forward. Then, when we were done, we emerged into the harsh light of day to implement those antiseptic plans.

Suddenly, I was faced with firing unbelievably competent, talented people as part of the strategies we arrived at in that sterile basement. It was a brutal time. In retrospect, I believe this experience sparked my commitment to helping people understand their strengths as a first step toward taking control of their destinies. You need to be able to chart your own course because your world can change in an instant. It was definitely during this time when such conversations became more commonplace for me.

In that moment, I understood without a doubt that it was not part of corporate DNA, any corporate DNA, to hold the hearts and minds of its employees at a premium. I say this with no hint of accusation whatsoever. The purpose of corporations is to create shareholder value.

**Creating individual success
rests in the hands of individuals.**

Nothing more. It's critical that you understand what they are and what they are not. While creating an employee-friendly workplace matters for recruiting and retaining talent, prioritizing the personal aspirations of employees above the needs of the organization is unrealistic. Putting your career first belongs to you. And make no mistake, the not-for-profit world is not some sacred, special place that puts a premium on its employees. A mission-driven organization is just that, mission-driven. Its goals are centered there, not on the personal aspirations of its employees. It may be pretty to think so, but really, such thinking is pretty idealistic and pretty foolish. Our markets are designed to create products and to create profits. Creating individual success rests in the hands of individuals.

IT'S ALL UP TO YOU.

The only person responsible for, and capable of, moving your personal mission forward is you. Denise Morrison, President and CEO of Campbell Soup Company, parent company of Bolthouse Farms, came to that realization early in her career. "By the time I was 30," she says, "I learned to be empowered about my own career. I thought; I can't rely on anybody else to do this for me. I need to do it myself."

And that's exactly how it should be. The only person who knows the reserves of energy, creativity, potential, drive, and passion buried deep inside of you, is you. If you don't care, if you don't try, who will? As I've said, if you don't want to try, why would anybody want to help you? But you're here. That's a start. As you take control of your life, as you have a better handle on yourself and your own life, you will be a better friend. Your interactions with people you care about will become more balanced, it will be easier for people to help you, and you'll have an easier time helping others. Your circle of friends will become stronger and possibly wider.

It does take courage to delve deeply into your strengths, aspirations, and wildest imaginings.

So nobody cares, and it's all up to you. Time to "screw your courage to the sticking place," to quote Lady Macbeth. It does take courage to delve deeply into your strengths, aspirations, and wildest imaginings. To acknowledge your unspoken fears, to give voice to your frustrations and your dreams, is not for the faint of heart. It's hard stuff. Sometimes it's painful stuff.

But are you really satisfied with the alternative?

Yes, living in the shadows is less taxing. That's why so many people do it. At first you will squint at the bright light of clarity. Yes, it's safer in the cave. Lots of people are there, all enabling you to simply accept a perfunctory level of happiness that is fine.

Fine.

Is there a more deflating white flag of truce than "fine"? How was your day? Fine. How was work? Fine. How are you? Fine. Flat. Easy. False.

Fine.

When is the last time you were fine? Today? Yesterday?

How were you really? Fine? Or maybe frustrated? Pissed off? Throwing up your hands in defeat? But your answer was "fine" because you didn't really want to share. It was complicated, messy, too much effort. It's a shield to hide behind to avoid the difficult work of fixing yourself. Fine.

HARD, BUT WORTH IT.

Yes, you'll find yourself facing 3 o'clock in the morning a lot. When you start the process of peeling back the layers, layers that haven't been touched in years, some people find that it's hard to decipher at first. What seems as if it should be simple and natural proves difficult because the investment is huge and the questions may feel brand new.

It's your battle to fight, your path to map, your truth to reveal. Your life.

There truly is no substitute for knowing yourself deeply and profoundly, for understanding what you want, for enabling you to pursue your own mission, for achieving the extraordinary, for being happier. It's your battle to fight, your path to map, your truth to reveal. Your life.

Only you know what's in your heart and in your mind. We all choose what parts of ourselves we will reveal to the people in our lives. The only person who knows all the pieces—who *can* know them all—is you. When you wake up in the middle of the night, only you know what first enters your mind, what keeps you from falling back asleep. When you sit in the drive-thru, waiting for your morning coffee, your daydreams are yours alone. All of these come together to define your essential truth, and understanding that is the first step to mapping the path to self-awareness, to fulfillment, to happiness. No one is more vested in you than you are, so what could feel better than recognizing that you control where you are going with your life? You're driving. You say where. You say when. You say how fast. Now, it's only a matter of programming the GPS.

As you prepare to start the SVP Exercise, to assume that nobody cares sets the right tone. You acknowledge who is in charge—and that is you. If you assume nobody really cares, it will actually set how you work through life in a more productive, proactive, and self-directed way. You will put yourself in charge and not sit around waiting for somebody else to save your ass, because 99.9% of the time they won't. And probably can't. So don't think they will. It will piss you off and just slow the process of advancing your personal mission and embracing a more fulfilling, happier life.

Somebody cares. You do.

DEFINE YOUR TRUTH AND MAP THE PATH AHEAD.

To Self-Awareness.

To Fulfillment.

To Happiness.

goals

WHERE DO YOU WANT TO GO?

Write it down.

Make it real.

Ask for what you want.

4
GOALS

"BE NOT AFRAID OF GREATNESS;
SOME ARE BORN GREAT, SOME ACHIEVE GREATNESS,
AND OTHERS HAVE GREATNESS THRUST UPON THEM."

William Shakespeare, *Twelfth Night*

It's all up to you, and you're ready. You've squared your shoulders. You can do this. Your homework starts now.

But for a moment, you think about literally writing your story and suddenly you are paralyzed by Julie Andrews' voice in your head telling you to "start at the very beginning," and seriously, how? Perhaps in singing the notes of "Do-Re-Mi" that is indeed "a very good place to start," but in this context, there's a fair argument to be made for exactly the opposite.

It's time to talk about your goals.

As you think about your personal story arc, it cannot move forward until one thing has occurred. You must, quite simply, decide where you want to go. You don't pull out of the driveway in the morning without knowing where you are headed, so it doesn't make sense to begin to move your career forward without some thought about direction.

IDENTIFY YOUR
SKILLS, VALUES,
PASSION

SET YOUR

goals

CREATE
YOUR STORY

APPLY
YOUR RESULTS

GETTING STUCK IS COMMON.

People often drift through life giving little thought to where they are going. It happens so easily, it very often goes unnoticed. You may recognize the pattern. You take a job. Begin a relationship. Perhaps start a family. You move to a job that better fits the parameters of your life. Your route becomes one of reacting to what's in front of you rather than purposefully pursuing what you want. And one day, you wake up and realize that you've drifted far from anything in your career that feels meaningful.

In the midst of an organizational change that sparked a great deal of introspection, a young colleague talked about his career path. His first job had been the outgrowth of an extracurricular involvement in college. He had moved forward nicely in his career, winning three promotions over a modest handful of years. But as the pending structural changes in the organization loomed before him, he realized that he had slipped rather aimlessly into his career. What had been meaningful to him several years ago now rang hollow, and he was at a loss for what to do next that would allow him to maintain his current salary level and remain in the same mid-sized town with a rather limited job market. He had no career goal he was able to communicate.

Part of self-awareness includes understanding the world around you. On a flight from New York, just as discussions about writing this book had begun, a young woman on the plane struck up a conversation. I had something to read, but Stephanie was sweet and personable and chatty. I never read a page. She had been in New York for medical school interviews. She talked about the interviews, about the people she met on campus, about volunteer work she had done as an undergraduate, and she described the kind of doctor she wanted to be. As she talked about the relationships she wanted to build with people and the depth of connection that was important to her, it seemed unlikely that becoming a doctor would fill her heart. She had set her sights on a goal, medical school, but the story for her life that she had built around it seemed disconnected from the goal itself.

> You must, quite simply, decide where you want to go.

A PLAN WILL EMPOWER YOU.

On the flip side of that is Campbell's CEO Denise Morrison. I've heard Denise talk a lot about the influence of her father and knowing since she was a young girl what she wanted to be when she grew up. "There was always a plan," she explains, "short-term, long-term. I knew I wanted to run a business because my father had definitely whetted my appetite about the joys and the challenges of business. But I had to have short-term goals. I was a very high achiever in terms of grades. That wasn't just for my parents. That was a scorecard for me, a personal review. Grades were always really, really important to me. I had to get A's and B's." It's worth noting that hers was an incredibly goal-oriented house. Her sister, Maggie Wilderotter served as CEO of Frontier Communications, and their other two sisters have had successful careers as well.

I'm not suggesting that you can only attain success if you've known since you were in elementary school what you wanted to be when you grew up. I do believe it's never too late to set a goal and pursue it. But I will say; the people I've met whose success is on par with that of Denise Morrison don't get to that point without a reasonable idea of the broad goals they want to achieve. Your objective is to get to your goal via as direct a path as possible. Life will throw you curve balls but don't get too stressed. No one has a perfectly linear path. The number of false starts, missteps, and course corrections you make will be reduced when you have a clear idea of where you are going and what you want.

For Denise, it was her father who was an influence on her career. As I mentioned, for me, it was my grandfather who drilled into me a sense of responsibility and an expectation of achievement. Pops was in my face most of the time. His intensity, along with playing sports, instilled a competitive drive in me when I was very young. All of that was reinforced in my first job out of Purdue at Procter & Gamble.

It's well-documented that P&G is "a promote from within" organization. Training, leadership development, an understanding of strengths and weaknesses, all were important parts of the P&G brand management environment. Every part of our world at P&G was tied to where you were and where you were going to be next within the organization. Having goals—one-year, five-year, with explicit, measurable outcomes and a sense of how to get there—was essential.

It seems that I've always been immersed in a world of goal orientation. From the time I was young, writing down my goals has been natural for me. In my mind, if I write it down, it becomes real, and I have to commit to it.

GRAB A NOTEBOOK. WRITE IT DOWN.

To me, that physical act of writing is an important thing. I spend plenty of time on my computer, my phone, my tablet. But when it's time to really read something, when it's time for the edits, I need paper and I need a pen. Handwriting is an important piece of how this story came together. Oh, there were countless hours spent on the laptop, but there are also notebooks, filled from front to back, capturing every phone conversation throughout the process. There are drafts with my notes and drawings that served as a reference along the way. Some of the most compelling notes came from our early readers, who scrawled in the margins and continued their insights to the back pages of the draft. Pen and paper. A Princeton University study found that students retain information better when they write their notes rather than type them into a computer. That makes perfect sense to me. Often, when trying to recall something, I see it in my mind's eye as part of the process of remembering. When that happens, more often than not, it is tied to my hand moving a pen across a page. Make notes as you work through this book, whether it's in the margins or in a notebook dedicated to finding your way to *Be More*. This is essential to completing your homework in a productive way.

In my mind, if I write it down, it becomes real, and I have to commit to it.

As you wrest control of your future back into your hands, it starts with setting goals and writing them down. Doing so allows you to start with the end in mind. Your story will become richer, and it will become easier for you to see the pieces coming together. You will also find that with explicitly stated goals, it will be easier to recognize and celebrate your successes along the way.

You should also recognize that, ironically, doing your job well also can inhibit your growth. When you are great at your job, people sometimes put you in a box. A situation evolves in which they can't imagine seeing you anywhere else—in part because to move you into a new position would be painful to them. In their eyes, you have become irreplaceable. The better you are; the more restricting that box can become. When this happens, it is incumbent upon you to say what you want, to say that staying in this box is no longer acceptable, to say that it's time for something more.

> You will also find that with explicitly stated goals, it will be easier to recognize and celebrate your successes along the way.

Denise Morrison points out that as a leader, understanding her employees' goals is important. "It's easier for your manager to take care of you if you know what you want. Your manager can provide the opportunities and be a catalyst for making things happen." All of that, she explains, is tied to helping people reach their potential. "You look at what the company can do to provide the opportunities for people to build their talents and contribute in a bigger way. At the same time, people need to think about what they want to do to improve themselves: Stretch, take bigger risks, be bolder about what they can do and how they can contribute. There's an enormous responsibility as a leader to provide those opportunities and to see people flourish."

It's *your* responsibility to know and be able to say what you want. No one can help you get what you want until you can ask them.

SET A GOAL TO MOVE YOURSELF FORWARD.

It's okay. Don't freak out. This isn't about establishing a goal for some epic, carved-in-granite, no-holds-barred endgame. Think of your goals as waypoints as you travel through life. There are many you've already set and accomplished: Graduating from high school, graduating from college, etc. The notion of setting a goal should not be paralyzing. It's merely the articulation of a next metric on your personal horizon. It may be a job title, it may involve recognition, or it may be financial. It should be specific, it should be measurable, it should be achievable. You might reach it, or it might shift along the way, and that's perfectly fine. Set a goal for six months from now, a year, five years. Know that you will revisit your goals and reassess them regularly. Goals are a fluid part of the exercise, touchstones that will spur your forward momentum and clarify your thinking.

People frequently become hamstrung about the idea of setting goals. Don't be. You have to start somewhere. For me, the goal was to be a leader in a Fortune 300 company. It was no more specific than that. I wanted scale, I wanted bigness. I didn't define it in terms of title. Your goals become more specific over time. But as you begin to think about getting what you want, it's important to have a North Star. Think vision, not precision.

As you start to think about your goals, be aware that many times the biggest obstacle to fulfilling your potential is you. People talk themselves out of greatness—and into indecision. I've seen it again and again. And perhaps the greatest tragedy is that it is often the smartest, most capable people who do this the most. It may be that their intelligence, their ability to foresee the possible complications associated with change, stymies them. It may be that as they work through the logistics of their options, see the costs associated with doing something new, they are unwilling to step into the unknown. Others start to work through the gap analysis and get lost there without ever reaching the other side. Finally, others talk and talk, but they never move. But it doesn't have to be this way. Recognize that decisions aren't black and white, that opportunities have costs, and that rewards are almost always accompanied by risk. It may seem as though there's no risk in the status quo, but never moving may result in the greatest cost

Think vision, not precision.

of all. As my colleague Bill Levisay notes, there's a point when you have to stop talking and start doing.

FIND AN EXAMPLE THAT INSPIRES YOU.

To begin the process of identifying your goals, think about others who have moved forward in ways that seem appealing to you. Consider a path that may not seem purposeful on the surface, but look harder. Often you will see a progression that seems meandering actually is linked by a deliberate thread. The perspective offered by hindsight may render the road taken by others more transparent, and thus help as you think about mapping your own. Of course, the serendipity of fortunate timing, and even luck, plays a role in many success stories.

It may seem as though there's no risk in the status quo, but never moving may result in the greatest cost of all.

There is perhaps no easier place to confirm that little bit of wisdom than in the Biographies aisle of your local bookstore. Look for biographies, autobiographies, and memoirs of individuals you admire. The subjects of these books may be connected to your field or to your interests. They may simply be individuals who have captured your imagination. You will be inspired by their successes, their responses to failure, their tenacity, and the bits of dumb luck that propelled them forward on their personal journeys.

Take a moment. Engage the imagination we talked about earlier. Imagine that the world unfolded in your way. Sit quietly or, if you prefer, take a walk—think about what that would look like.

Let's turn to Shakespeare and the words that started this chapter. Set aside the very small percentage who are "born great." It's a good bet they aren't reading this book. Set aside as well those who have had "greatness thrust upon them." There have been accidents of history and of fate that tested the mettle of individuals and lay bare a sometimes breathtaking greatness. The intent here is not to send you tilting at windmills in pursuit of some epic heroism. That leaves us with those who "achieve greatness," individuals no different than you and I who excel not through some accident of birth or circumstance but through personal achievement. This is your opportunity space. Your task is to create the circumstance that allows you to exhibit the distinctive capacity for greatness that already exists within you.

When I think of my earliest idol, Walter Cronkite, I see greatness. Man, I loved Walter Cronkite. I watched him every night. Thanks to YouTube, his seminal moments, the ones I was too little to remember well, are available for all of us to see. To watch video of Cronkite reporting the death of President Kennedy is riveting. He didn't only report the news; he lived the moment with us. His despair was our despair. Reporting the moon landing, his almost childlike joy was our joy. I wouldn't have been able to explain it then, but looking back, I see in him a perfect alignment of skills, values, and passion that turned him into one of the most iconic figures in American history, the quintessential communicator.

We can fast forward to find contemporary examples. Think about two men who achieved greatness and created impact at the highest level: Steve Jobs and Bill Gates. There is no doubt that both men were blessed with exceptional intelligence. But how much more intelligent were they, was even Cronkite really, than you or I? The source of their greatness is not simply a marker of intelligence. Rather, I believe the source of their greatness, the breadth of their transformative achievement, resulted from an uncanny alignment of skills, values, and passion all pointed toward goals they wanted to achieve.

FINDING YOUR INTERSECTION OF SKILLS, VALUES, AND PASSION.

Imagine melding the intersection of your skills, values, and passion so that your work became deeply ingrained in your being. Imagine that you consistently immersed yourself in it so completely that you lost all track of time. Imagine a future in which your work became such an integral part of you that you could not envision your life without it. It's not some special purview of a select few to be able to do so. I believe that for the majority of people, what you love, in whatever form, is what you could be doing in a productive, value-creating way.

When people find a way to work at the intersection of their skills, values, and passion, it changes the entire work environment. I've discussed these issues many times with my former colleague Peter Kaye, presently Food Science Chief Marketing Officer of NuTek. "It is totally different," he explains. "It's a little hard to articulate. I think it manifests itself in terms of work ethic, whether it be hours worked or frequency of checking your email. The more you're into your job, it doesn't feel like a job. You're reading about your industry, your competition, and you don't think 'Why am I doing this at 9 o'clock at night?' You just do it because you want to. You think, 'I'm gonna work hard because I want this to be really great.'"

My best friend, Rusty Rueff, built his career in human resources in top positions at PepsiCo and Electronic Arts. Now a board member at Glassdoor and HireVue, he continues to be a leader when it comes to workplace trends. In an interview for *MarketWatch* about job satisfaction and productivity, he captures the deep commitment that Peter is talking about. "We've all been in places where we've pulled all-nighters, and we're going back to the pizza box for the second time, and the pizza's cold," he says. "You sort of hate that you're there, but at the same time there's nowhere else you'd rather be."

I've found all of that over the past few years at Bolthouse Farms. It's by far the most significant thing I've ever done. Our CEO Jeff Dunn brought me in with a goal of transforming a commodity carrot company into a place that would influence the national conversation about how we eat. We've made a fantastic difference in terms of creating a contemporary brand and evolving into a company that sets the tone in the produce industry. That fueled our ability to step into the White House and participate in policy conversations in a big way, starting with Sam Kass, when he led the *Let's Move!* organization. And all of that comes from being a mission-centered organization. It is the heart of our success. Setting the mission changed the gravitational pull of the whole company. All of that is a function of knowing who we are, what we mean to people, and what we mean to ourselves. We tell our story in everything we do in a way that is authentic and creates impact. Every bit of that happened because Jeff Dunn had a vision of good for Bolthouse Farms and an unwavering commitment to achieving it.

In fact, that story was so powerful that after Campbell Soup Company acquired Bolthouse Farms, CEO Denise Morrison became intrigued by our mission and wanted to inspire Campbell's employees and customers in a similar way. That gave me the opportunity to work with Denise to help architect the new Campbell's purpose, "Real Food that Matters for Life's Moments." It's a bold step for one of the country's largest food producers to adopt a purpose statement about focusing on making food that's good, honest, and real and that benefits consumers. Having experienced the impact of redefining our mission at Bolthouse Farms, I know that it promises to recast Campbell in a meaningful way as well.

YOUR GOAL IS WHAT'S TRUE TO YOU.

None of this is to say that guiding you to your intersection of skills, values, and passion is intended to make you work around the clock or that your goal needs to change the world. It's not. But the fact is, you spend a significant portion of your waking hours on the job, even if you work a straight 8-to-5. Shouldn't the place where you spend such a significant part of your life feel true to what matters to you? Shouldn't the job that in many ways defines you, do so in a way that you choose and reflects the things that you value?

Karen McCullough, a development and stewardship director for the Purdue Research Foundation, talks about completing the SVP Exercise and taking steps to better align her professional and personal lives. For Karen, a mother of two small daughters with a third child on the way, finding balance as the primary family breadwinner was critical. "I envision a career where I am able to become an 'expert' and orchestrate successes during the day. My values *insist* that I keep my work separate from the rest of my life," she explains. "It's stellar to have an exercise like this that opens your eyes and inspires you to make small changes— enough to find fulfillment. Completing the exercise also highlighted for me the things about my *current* job that were *already working*, things that were already advancing me toward a goal that was good, along a meaningful path. The SVP Exercise helped me to tune in to, celebrate, and emphasize those aspects of my job that were already in alignment with my SVP."

Hitting the target to align your skills, values, and passion in pursuit of a goal with the same precision that propelled Cronkite, Jobs, and Gates is no easy task. Their abiding belief in and commitment to their work appears extraordinary. Few of us will ever match their exceptional alignment of skills, values, and passion. But the mere fact of diligently trying to do so will move you toward finding work that allows you to create a life that is more authentically yours.

As you consider your goals and all you want to achieve, don't shy away from your greatest imaginings. Don't limit the scope of your dreams because you can't yet see how to achieve them. Jobs famously said, "You can't connect the dots looking forward; you can only connect them looking backwards." That doesn't mean you shouldn't move forward deliberately. At the same time, the limits of what you know at the precise moment that you are reading these words should not be a factor that limits your potential. We all learn, grow, and evolve every day. If your goals illuminate a shortfall, use that knowledge to acquire the skills, the connections, and the wherewithal to move toward your goal in a very deliberate fashion. As Olympic alpine skier Picabo Street said, "To uncover your true potential, you must first find your own limits,

> Take a deep breath and have the courage to step into yourself and all that you want to accomplish.

and then you have to have the courage to blow past them." Take a deep breath and have the courage to step into yourself and all that you want to accomplish.

Green Bay Packers Coach Vince Lombardi, in a famous locker room speech, argued that football, like life, is a game of inches. In his analogy, the difference between winning and losing, between being a champion and an also-ran, may be only half a step. There may be little more than half a step between you and achieving your goals, between you and greatness. With a little more persistence, finding your truth, articulating your mission, and achieving more in your life may be closer than you ever imagined.

So dream big. Then act.

SET GOALS TO PUSH YOUR LIMITS, TO BE MORE.

Be Purposeful.

Embrace Greatness.

Dream Big.

skills

MAKE A LIST OF YOUR EXCEPTIONAL SKILLS:

What do you do best?

What do people most admire about you?

What sets you apart?

5
SKILLS

**"KNOWING YOURSELF IS THE
BEGINNING OF ALL WISDOM."**

Aristotle

You've identified a goal and have some sense of where you want to go. Now, it's time to look in the mirror and assess the skills you have that will get you there.

It's been a nice little ride to this point in the book. You've thought about some things that made you squirm a bit. You're thinking a little harder and deeper about yourself than you have for a long time.

The homework gets real now. Grab your notebook again, reach for your favorite pen. Go for the purple ink. It's quirky, and it will cheer you when the words in front of you—or even worse, those you can't muster to even write on the page—make you want to pull out your hair. Remember when we talked about how it's all up to you, that "nobody cares" part? Well now, with a goal in mind, it's time to get busy. It's time to do the work so you can develop your plan.

Five skills. That's the assignment.

This is an exercise about your career, so we're talking about the skills you take to the workplace. Also, this is a way to identify those things about you that are exceptional. It's not a comprehensive data dump of every single thing you can do. It's an exploration of those things you do best and that set you apart. Think about what people say about you. What skills are consistently mentioned when people talk about the special contributions you make? What are the consistent highlights of your annual performance review? Write those down. Don't worry; it's OK if the initial list is more than five. As you review and find the best way to say what you mean, it will become easier to condense the list to your five exceptional skills.

What skills are consistently mentioned when people talk about the special contributions you make?

EVERYONE ADDS VALUE.

Before we really dive in, remember, don't get bogged down in what skills you have or don't have. It's a big world out there with room for people of all types. There's no wrong answer here as long as it's true to you. The market economies exist and support all of the things we do. Goods, services, and skills have different monetary values attached, but be assured, everyone has something to contribute.

That message was delivered loud and clear while I was a teenager working in the oil fields with Pops. I was always given the worst jobs there. Whether it was painting one oil rig after another, slapping up blue or yellow paint over the most recent layer of filth, shoving my arm into a hole filled with this viscous mud, or smelling, literally, for natural gas or oil to see if we were getting into a vein of it. The work was hard, and it was dirty.

One day when I was maybe 16, Pops drove up in his new Oldsmobile. Every year there was a new Olds or a new Buick—never a Caddy—but always something new. I was covered with dirt, I was frustrated, and I got in his face, challenging him, asking why I had to do this job when my name was on the company. He stepped toward me and shoved me back, down into a muddy pool. As I lay in the muck, propped up on my elbows, Pops had a lot of choice words for me. But these are the ones I still remember decades later. "You are no better than anybody else on the planet." Then he just walked away. We all bring value, we do it in different ways, but everybody counts.

I carried that lesson with me to Procter & Gamble. Among my cohort of 93 new employees, 90 held master's degrees in business. Just three of us were straight out of undergrad. With a degree in communication, I was the only one with a liberal arts background. At first I was petrified because everyone around me knew things I couldn't even fake. Some of those people could dive so deeply into an Excel spreadsheet that they could hardly find their way out. For me, the broader strokes were more important than the minutia. My objective wasn't to master the spreadsheet. I took the skills I had, a combination of real-world practicality and the creativity to see things differently, and put my all into it. I wasn't going to roll over, and I wasn't going to be something I was not. If I was going to fail, I was going to do it at top speed. What I learned, and what they learned, is that the liberal arts guy brought something to the organization that the "too smart to ride a bike" business types simply could not. I embraced who I was and what I knew, and it worked because I had an opposite, but complementary, set of skills. It was a big deal for me when I was the seventh person in that group to be promoted.

The point? The world needs all manner of talent. My experience at P&G proved that a diversity of skills is essential in the workplace. Understand who you are and what you bring to the table, and then use these to your best advantage. There's no set of skills that doesn't have application, that isn't valued. Be exactly who you are, at your best. When you embrace yourself and your unique strengths, the success that follows will validate you and your truth. It's the place where people who have found an intersection of skills, values,

Be exactly who you are, at your best.

and passion blossom. "A winner," says basketball legend Larry Bird, "is someone who recognizes his God-given talents, works his tail off to develop them into skills, and uses those skills to accomplish his goals."

JUST START THE CONVERSATION.

Dave was a young graphic designer without a real ability to articulate his skills when I started working with him. But he was ready to move onto something bigger and immediately initiated a conversation with me about his career. Our discussion resulted in him working through the SVP exercise.

> ✳ As you begin to write a list of your skills, also write why these are your particular strengths. This will help you clarify your five exceptional skills.

"It seemed like it was almost too simple of an exercise at first," remembers Dave. "It ended up being three or four rounds. You said, 'List your skills, values, passion, and come back to me in a week.' You also said, 'I'm going to challenge you, so make sure you believe it, and it's all true.'" He explains, "I listed my skills and wrote a short paragraph of how each skill applied to me. I felt like for every word I put on that page, I had to be able to back it up. For me, it was really trying because one of my values is integrity, and I felt like I needed to own every single word."

Finding his truth was a tougher part of the SVP homework than Dave had anticipated. "It was surprising how taxing it was on my brain," he laughs. "It was really challenging. That's kind of the interesting thing about it. I thought, what I'm doing is not really a complex thing.... Listing them out, it's a simple thing as far as coming up with them. But for so long, sorting through all the noise and the thoughts and dealing with this, I found it's very challenging to say what I'm really good at and what I want to do."

For Julie Soley, from the consumer relations area at Bolthouse Farms, the challenge was a bit different. "I'm not the type of person used to putting so much spotlight on myself," she explains. "For me, that's been the hardest thing—to really take a look at myself. I'm so used to taking care of other people, but I'm not used to taking a look at myself and what I'm doing."

Before we move ahead, let me take a moment to emphasize this. As I said earlier in our discussion of goals, the act of writing things down is an integral part of this exercise. Don't think you can move forward just doing this in your head. You can't. "It's absolutely the tangible act of writing it down and seeing it on paper that makes it real," agrees my former colleague Jack. "That holds true for so many things. You need to bring it out of your head and into the world." It's true. Once it's on that piece of paper or flickering on a computer screen, it stares back at you. It challenges you. It creates a commitment that becomes real.

> **Don't think you can move forward just doing this in your head. You can't.**

Moving on, to help generate your list, let's talk about skills under a few broad categories and think about the different ways your strengths may connect. All of these are valued skills in the workplace, and knowing where you stand out is an important part of understanding how to direct your life and career to be more productive, more successful, and it often follows, more empowered and happier.

Remember, this list is a starting point. It's not comprehensive, but it should help you think about how to pinpoint your particular skills.

PERFORM A SKILLS INVENTORY.

☐ *Leader*

Are you a Pied Piper who can inspire groups of people to move in particular directions? Do you lead by example in a way that makes those around you work better? Do you have a noteworthy ability to manage people and enable them to fulfill their potential? Do you find yourself at the helm more often than not when work on a new project begins? Do you always raise your hand and find it hard to hold back?

☐ *Communicator*

Communication skills can take myriad forms. Are you an exceptional writer? An inspiring speaker? Do you have a particular ability to speak in front of large groups? Do you have the finesse to position your organization to its best advantage?

☐ *Team Member/Soloist*

Are you energized by being part of a group? Does collaboration fuel your creativity and commitment? Or are you more comfortable working on a task by yourself and delivering the finished product on your own?

☐ *Problem Solver*

When disaster ensues, are you the person others look to for a tempered response? Do you exhibit courage and grace under pressure and deal effectively with conflict?

☐ *Adaptable/Flexible*

Are you open to new ideas and generally able to cope well when things don't go as planned?

☐ *Strategic Thinker*

Do you envision the successful endgame and have the ability to work backward, identifying and marshalling the components necessary to achieve your vision? Does your brain connect the dots to bring pieces together to initiate new realities?

☐ *Personal/Interpersonal*

Do you have a special knack for one-on-one interactions that allows you to make significant personal connections? Does your ability to relate allow you to manage diverse relationships and politically sensitive situations with aplomb? Do you have a memorable personality and an empathy that deepens your relationships?

☐ *Analytical*

Are you a critical and logical thinker with a penchant for facts and figures? Do you revel in solving problems? Are you adept at breaking things down to understand their essential components and relations as a way of envisioning solutions and developing a plan for making systems work together? Do reason and logic guide your thought processes?

☐ *Detail Oriented*
  Are you the person who moves a project from Point A to Point B, with the operating skills and ability to delegate that keeps people on point and organized, assuring a project moves seamlessly from start to finish?

☐ *Integrity/Work Ethic*
  Do honor and trustworthiness guide your interactions with coworkers and customers? Do you take a particular pride in your work and have a commitment to stay on task until the job is done?

☐ *Innovator/Creator*
  Do you excel in bringing new ideas and challenges to the forefront? Do you specialize in thinking outside the box and moving beyond the status quo? Are you the Big Idea person with a gift for conceptual thinking?

☐ *Curious*
  Do you thrive on learning new things? Does the demand to do something different excite you? Are you easily bored and always yearning for the next challenge?

☐ *Negotiator*
  Are you particularly adept at developing agreements and bringing parties together to create mutually desirable outcomes and sustain long-term relationships?

☐ *Conflict Manager*
  Do you have the ability to assess a situation patiently and use the right words, tone, and nonverbal cues to communicate clearly and effectively even when tensions are high?

☐ *Persuasive*
  Do you have a knack for getting what you want? Is your special skill tied to the ability to make a case, know your audience, and pitch your argument so that people feel compelled to consider your point of view and often find themselves wanting the same outcome that you do?

As you consider this list, think deeply about what skills reflect your unique value. Be honest. Recognize that some pairs of skills don't make logical sense. Don't forget, you can only choose five. This isn't a laundry list of everything you can do. It's an itemization of those skills that elevate you above the crowd, those things other people admire in you, those places where you excel. It represents how others in your family, school, workplace, and community see you. Also, know that over the course of your career, your skills will change and grow. They will become more sophisticated, and you may develop particular depth in one or two of the broad areas noted above in a manner that differentiates you in a big way in terms of your particular set of skills. Use the list as a guide—a starting point for the self-reflection that will allow you to assess yourself in a genuine way.

RECOGNIZE YOUR EVOLVING SKILLS.

Eric Johnson, another former colleague from Coca-Cola, remembers a discussion we had early in his career: "You told me, 'There's no one I would rather have leading the team up the hill than you.' That was a good 14 years ago. But after that, you said, 'Next, you need to go figure out which hill you need to be taking.' That's a conversation I remember a lot." It was, Eric says, about making the transition from lieutenant to general, something that has evolved over the course of his career. "I've always had a drive for results, an action orientation, that over time has evolved to a bit more of thoughtfulness, a strategic planning perspective." It has been terrific to watch Eric step into leadership roles in a big way.

At various points in your career, circumstances will offer unexpected opportunities. When that happens, don't be afraid to take risks. When I look back at my grandfather, I am reminded of his pragmatic way of assessing risks. For him, calculated risks resulted in a lot of success. Don't hesitate to push yourself, to make yourself a little uncomfortable. In that moment, you will find that a willingness to step into a new role, to move beyond your fears, can create a situation that allows you to stretch and more clearly see the unique set of skills that you have to offer.

LISTEN TO WHAT OTHERS HAVE TO SAY.

As part of this process, gather input from others around you. Ask people who are close enough to you to be truthful and agree or disagree with your assessment. Consider other perspectives on your work and your strengths. How you are perceived matters a great deal. An understanding of how others assess your work helps you see your skills more clearly, and it allows you to highlight the skills that matter most to you in a more deliberate way. If there's something that you believe is an exceptional skill and no one around you sees it, you have a problem. You need to determine whether your assessment is off, or if you aren't doing a good job of conveying your work and your particular skills to those around you. In either case, you should address this disconnect.

As you pull the list together, don't compile it in a scattershot way. If you have them, look closely at your performance reviews to determine your strengths as consistently noted by your supervisor. The five skills you identify represent half of the homework you will use to write your personal story. From a job standpoint, your skills are paramount. What you choose to focus on matters a great deal. It will direct your next thing in a significant way as you move toward finding your truth and defining the work that advances your mission.

Consider deeply. Request input.

UNDERSTAND THE SKILLS THAT ELEVATE YOU ABOVE THE CROWD.

Think Deeply.

Be Honest.

Seek Input.

values

WHAT ARE THE VALUES THAT DRIVE YOUR DECISION MAKING?

What responsibilities guide your actions?

What motivates and inspires you?

What shapes how you move in your world?

6

VALUES

"YOU STILL, IN A VERY FUNDAMENTAL WAY, ARE WHAT
YOU BELIEVE IN. YOUR LIFE IS STILL DEFINED BY HOW YOU
SEE YOUR OBLIGATIONS, YOUR RESPONSIBILITIES, AND WHETHER
YOUR HAPPINESS IS ROOTED IN THE WELL-BEING OF OTHERS
AS WELL AS YOURSELF."

Bill Clinton, *Closing Remarks, Health Matters January 2014*

If creating a list of your five skills demanded a hard look in the mirror, identifying your four core values requires a profound look at yourself and your relationship with everything you care about most in the world.

For the SVP Exercise, values represent the things in your life that are most important to you, whether you are consciously aware of them or not. They will define you and factor into your decision making at a practical, day-to-day level. These are the things that are important to you and true to what you think, what you believe, how you act, how you live. That's a key point. Your values determine not what you say you will do, but the actions that follow your words. When you listen to your gut, it's very likely that your values are quietly guiding your actions. While our larger exercise is tied to career, it's critical you understand that values are not directly about your vocation. Your skills will change and grow through the years; however, your values are a part of your essential being and don't tend to change much over time.

At this point, you might be asking, "But if this is about knowing myself, creating a more fulfilling career, and identifying some elusive intersection of skills and passion, what do my values have to do with it?"

The objective here is to understand yourself better—to know what you're good at, what you care about, what energizes you. Taken together, SVP aims to provide you the tools to take a comprehensive look at yourself in order to find your personal intersection of skills, values, and passion. Taking that extra step—looking beyond skills and beyond passion, and exploring your values—provides a litmus test to gauge whether it will all work for you in your world. Absent that, you could find yourself shooting for a target that's completely incongruent with your life outside work. And that won't get you anywhere productive over the long haul.

> **Your values determine not what you say you will do, but the actions that follow your words.**

VALUES DEFINE WHAT MATTERS MOST TO YOU.

I was nearing thirty before the importance of values became clear to me. Goals, skills, those were always easy for me to identify. But late in my tenure at Procter & Gamble, I began to see people around me making career decisions that were based on other things. Love and family emerged as significant career drivers among people in my sphere. That's when I realized there was this really important piece of the dynamic to take into account. It's when the V entered SVP.

On the flip side, you need to realize companies don't hire based upon skills alone. If it were that simple, any automaton would do. Skills are only part of what you bring to the job. Sitting around the table, you'll never see a mere listing of competencies. Sitting around the table, you'll see people. The ones you like, the ones who inspire, the ones you wish would stop showing up because they are so damn annoying. And don't forget, the ones doing the hiring—they are people as well. In making hiring decisions, they look for people who have passion, who are articulate, whose values align closely with the organization, and who know who they are. Enumerating your values allows you to express yourself in a way that is compelling, honest, and true.

That's equally important for you and for the places you will work. Corporate culture (or organizational culture) reflects the collective values of the people inside, and particularly those leading, an organization. Your fit within the workplace, an integral driver of both your happiness and in all likelihood your success, is enormously significant.

YOUR VALUES DETERMINE YOUR JOB FIT.

Jeff Crow points to the importance of intangibles for determining how well a potential employee will fit with his group. In interviews, understanding who a person is outside of work is important. "I only need 10 or 15 minutes to decide if the person is competent," he explains. "I need twice that time to decide if they are a good fit. At some point, it's not the answers to the questions. I'm more concerned with how a person is saying things. I try to get to what's important to that person from a personal standpoint. I've never interviewed people and not asked 'when you're not at work, how do you like to spend your time?' I just like to see whether or not someone will get excited about something. I don't want someone who is only a workaholic. I want to see a passion for something."

"Fit is really important in any kind of environment," Jeff continues. "There's always a wide range of people who could do the job from the simple skills standpoint. But they've got to be the right fit. You've got to have the right person in the right place."

Jeff is right. In my experience, the number of people who leave jobs because they don't fit with the team is similar to the number who leave due to shortfalls in their skills or knowledge. This is a critical point. Your ability to know who you are, and to both express and project that, can save you a lot of heartache and false starts along the way.

While your skills define what you bring to the enterprise in a tangible, measurable way, your values differentiate who you are as a human being. In the midst of everything that represents your distinctive contribution, values epitomize a purely human part of your story. We talked about the variety of people around the table at work. Your values tell a great

Your ability to know who you are, and to both express and project that, can save you a lot of heartache and false starts along the way.

deal about the person you are. As you consider your four core values, it's important to think about those categories broadly. These are the things that drive your decision-making. Multiple pieces may fall under each category, capturing various aspects of the values that define you.

IT'S NOT WHAT YOU SAY. IT'S WHAT YOU DO.

It's vitally important to be honest. There can be a disconnect between our values and those things we think we should value. Think of it this way: There's some cachet attached to listening to public radio. We should if we're smart, engaged, in touch, right? But maybe your drive to work is energized by '90s grunge rock. There's an impulse to gravitate toward the socially respected notion that you envision for yourself rather than what you really do in the car by yourself. If you want to find your path to fulfillment, embrace your truth. It's what matters most, and it may even surprise you.

A 2010 study in the journal *Psychology of Popular Media Culture* notes a propensity among Facebook users to share an inordinate number of positive stories in comparison to what they would in "real life" interactions. The results found that Facebook users have a tendency to negatively compare themselves and their lives with those of their peers. This loops back to our early conversation about the truth of ourselves as we present it through social media.

"To live is to choose," said former United Nations Secretary General Kofi Annan. "But to choose well, you must know who you are and what you stand for, where you want to go, and why you want to get there." When you understand and acknowledge the values that drive your decision making, you will be better prepared to purposefully plot a course that is true to what matters most in your world.

If you want to find your path to fulfillment, embrace your truth.

FIND YOUR TRUTH.

"The exercise gave me a little bit more of a holistic perspective," says Eric Johnson. "As I was growing up and starting to have children, I told my wife I didn't really have time for children. That didn't go over too well. I had to get past that idea of kind of working tirelessly. You've got to be good at a lot of stuff, not just work, good as a husband, good as a father, good as a friend. Relationships were just not one of my priorities. But having worked through this exercise, engaging in life more fully has become an important thing for me."

Over the past five years or so, being part of a mission-centered, passion-led world has been an important component of my values. At Bolthouse Farms, with its commitment to healthy eating, and working in conjunction with Sam Kass and First Lady Michelle Obama's *Let's Move!* organization and the Partnership for a Healthier America, I've come in contact with a lot of people who are telling their stories in very powerful ways. It's become a real proof point to be among the people working on that issue. I have seen the degree to which knowing and working toward a mission that matters to them, that is in sync with their values, results in more productivity, more value creation, and often, simply makes these people happier. In my estimation, adding the values component to a discussion of skills and passion makes it a lot easier to get into that mission-centered, passion-led space.

It's important to point out that Procter & Gamble, too, is a mission-centered kind of place. Before anyone was talking in those terms, P&G

displayed an uncompromising commitment to doing the right thing. That commitment continues to run deep there. In fact, it was such a given, such an integral part of the company culture, that there was never a mission statement that touched upon those guideposts. The commitment was unquestioningly assumed.

THINK ABOUT VALUES.

As you consider this part of the SVP Exercise, it is worth noting that for many people, family will be among the four values noted. Other values, and this list is by no means comprehensive, might include:

☐ Integrity

☐ Geography

☐ Spirituality/religion

☐ Security

☐ Loyalty

☐ Power

☐ Work ethic

☐ Risk tolerance

☐ Work/life balance

☐ Pace

☐ Love of adventure vs. an affinity for the predictable

☐ Financial rewards

☐ Personal acclaim

✳ **As you begin to write a list of your values, also write what each value means in your life. This will help you articulate your four core values.**

You may find your values from among this list or you may move in different directions. Again, this is about *you*. There are no wrong answers, but there are answers that may not represent your truth. Embracing yourself, your authentic self, is the only way to complete this part of the exercise. If you aren't honest here, the personal story you write at the end of this process won't ring true to you. And then, really, what's the point?

> Embracing yourself, your authentic self, is the only way to complete this part of the exercise.

As you prepare to write down your four values, you need to think deeply about what each one means.

If family, for instance, is among your four values, what does that mean to you in practical terms? Is it about your parents? Siblings? Spouse? Children? So what? Does your family impact where you want to live? Does family affect the level of responsibility and time commitment associated with your ideal job? How does your commitment to family factor into the amount of financial compensation you need? And do your family obligations alter your list of preferred employers?

REACH BENEATH THE SURFACE TO FIND YOUR MEANING.

Our values are like icebergs. A small, obvious, predictable, and expected part is above the surface for all to see. But what each of your values means is tied to your life situation and all of the implications associated with it. That part below the surface makes it personal, makes it real, makes it yours, makes it matter. Your values are about what's in your heart. They represent the responsibility you carry with you every moment of every day. They motivate you and shape the way you approach the world. The things you value inspire you. Perhaps more than anything else, your values are where your ultimate fulfillment in the world lives.

To be clear, this isn't about baring yourself to the world. But it may well be about baring your thoughts, feelings, fears, and aspirations to yourself in a way you haven't before. You aren't gearing up to share every aspect of your values and what they mean with a lifetime of potential employers. That said, when you understand your values and know the implications of what they mean, you will be better positioned to evaluate opportunities in a way that will resonate within the context of your life. Our careers are a huge part of our lives. The time we devote to them alone makes that apparent. But they are only a part. Finding a career that complements both your skills and your values will move you in a positive way toward advancing your mission and achieving more fulfillment.

Recognize what matters most to you. Step toward the life you want.

**RECOGNIZE THE VALUES THAT SHAPE
THE WAY YOU APPROACH THE WORLD.**

Be Authentic.

Know Yourself.

Express Yourself.

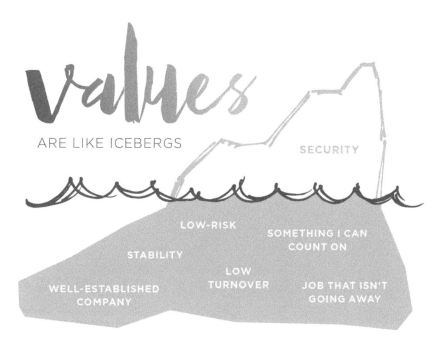

values

ARE LIKE ICEBERGS

SECURITY

LOW-RISK

SOMETHING I CAN
COUNT ON

STABILITY

LOW
TURNOVER

WELL-ESTABLISHED
COMPANY

JOB THAT ISN'T
GOING AWAY

Passion

WHAT IS YOUR INDISPENSABLE FUEL?

What makes your heart sing?

What puts you on your soapbox?

What could you lose yourself in for half a day?

7
PASSION

"I'VE LEARNED THAT PEOPLE WILL FORGET WHAT YOU SAID,
PEOPLE WILL FORGET WHAT YOU DID, BUT PEOPLE WILL
NEVER FORGET HOW YOU MADE THEM FEEL."

Maya Angelou, Poet

Here it is, finally. The passion question.

If you're in tune with your passion, engaged with it, you won't be able to stop talking about it, because you'll be, you know, passionate about it.

If Skills are your Brain and Values are your Heart, then Passion is your Soul. It evokes the visceral feeling of a literal fullness of your heart, a rush of adrenaline, a swell of emotion that energizes and completes you like nothing else. It is solely, unabashedly, and uncompromisingly about you alone and your reaction/response to it, regardless of the outside world. If values embody everything around you in your life, passion is what exists deep inside you. Strip everything else away, and passion remains. Passion, perhaps more than any other element, defines your path to genuine happiness, and if we are being honest, passion conveys the truest manifestation of your personal essence.

IF SKILLS ARE YOUR *brain*

AND VALUES ARE YOUR *heart*

THEN PASSION IS YOUR *soul*

A 2010 study published in the *Journal of Positive Psychology* followed "engaged living" youth, who were defined as those with a passion to help others and be completely immersed in activities. The study found that youths with higher levels of engaged living were more grateful, hopeful, happier, and generally more successful in school. So there it is, even science suggests passion is integral to your happiness.

DEFINING PASSION.

If your passion is an activity—music, art, extreme sports, canoeing, knitting—it should be fairly easy for you to write it on that piece of paper in front of you. If, on the other hand, it is something amorphous, it might be difficult to capture it in words. If you fall into that camp, it may help to talk more about passion.

To be clear, music, art, extreme sports—none of those is passion in and of itself. They are only activities. Passion is a fundamentally human emotion, and it is only the feelings these activities evoke in individuals who engage in them that elevates them to the level of passion. Passion lives in the individual, not the activity. It is the intense emotion, overarching enthusiasm, and compelling zeal which people bring to an action that makes it noteworthy.

For me, the concept of passion started to come into play during my time at Coca-Cola. When you get right down to it, that's really what Coke sells. In terms of product, it's flavored water—nothing more. But when you think about Coca-Cola it's not the product, it's the advertising that resonates. "It's the Real Thing" and "I'd like to teach the world to sing." The emotion tied to those messages is inspiring. It gives you goose bumps. That's the genius of their marketing; they sell a feeling, an ethos. At Coca-Cola, we talked a lot about passion, emotion. We spent a lot of time trying to understand people's passions. The power of that began to show me in a tangible way just how important and influential personal passion can be.

Passion lives in the individual, not the activity.

That's probably what made me begin to think about my passion. I can't pinpoint exactly when I was first able to articulate it, but I can look back and see that it's been there all along. I can look back to the sixth grade and see it. My extraordinary passion is leading people, understanding what makes them tick, and making the whole thing move forward. I love organizing a better mission. I love the idea of leading a group of talented people and pushing them farther than they think they can go. Passion is the third leg on the stool that completes the SVP Exercise. It completes the picture and makes the elements of the Exercise balance in a way that integrates your aspiration alongside your talents and what matters to you. To me, taken together, it feels really right.

Julie Soley, from Bolthouse Farms, who spent many years focused on her son, said this was the toughest part of her homework. "This was painful. This was really hard for me because I don't have hobbies. There isn't anything that I would say when someone asks me, 'What is your passion?' outside of my family. That led me to thinking: 'Why don't I have hobbies?' I think a lot of it comes from being a single mom. All of those years were focused on my child." As she sifted through those thoughts, she was able to point to her passion. "What I finally ended up with," she says, "is helping others. That's what drives me, whether it's my family, or helping my team be more successful, or working in the local rescue mission." Once she reached below the surface, Julie identified her passion and could see ways to apply it in many parts of her life.

YOUR PASSION LETS YOU SHINE.

Once you gain that awareness, you'll realize passion is what sets you apart. Passion is breathtaking to experience—and even breathtaking to witness. In the arts and in sports, some moments embody passion. We've all seen it, a melding of the actor with her character in which the two are so completely intertwined, it is as though they've become one. We've also seen those moments in sports: Reggie Miller scoring eight points in 8.9 seconds in a playoff game or Brett Favre's spectacular Monday Night Football performance the day after his father died. We know we have seen something exceptional: An individual fully immersed in his passion.

Those moments are inspiring, and they are memorable. They have the ability to give us chills vicariously as we see and are moved by the expression of passion in others. Passion is the antithesis of apathy; in its presence, it is all but impossible to look away. It **Passion attracts.** is mesmerizing, magnetic, indelible. The energy is so palpable that even as spectators, we feel it. By extension, that energy makes people who share their passion compelling and electric. Passion attracts.

The *Urban Dictionary* offers a great definition. "Passion is when you put more energy into something than is required to do it." (Think about that. If you know the feeling, follow that thought to your passion.) *UD* continues, "It is more than just enthusiasm or excitement. Passion is ambition that is materialized into action to put as much heart, mind, body, and soul into something as is possible."

Think about that: "Passion is ambition that is materialized into action."

WHAT LIGHTS YOU UP?

You really only have one passion. It may be connected to your vocation, or it may not. Nevertheless, recognizing and articulating your passion can light your path in a way that will be meaningful to you. It may line up with your skills and values, or it may complement those in a way that is uncommonly yours. Passion is the free spirit of this process, and quite possibly, the essence of your free spirit. It is that thing that makes your heart sing.

> Passion is the free spirit of this process,
> and quite possibly, the essence of your free spirit.

It may even make you sing, or at least speak with a bit of a lilt. In a 2014 article in *The Chronicle of Higher Education*, Joli Jensen, Hazel Rogers Professor of Communication at the University of Tulsa, talks about the importance of faculty and students bringing their passion into their research. She notes that as people talk about things that matter to them and that they are passionate about, it's possible to hear a musical "lilt" in their voices. In an exercise for one of her classes, students present three options for their senior project. Collectively, classmates listen for the lilt in each presenter's voice as part of helping identify the project that will be the most engaging to each student. As you talk through this part of your SVP homework with family and friends, ask them to listen for that lilt as part of helping you identify your passion.

For Peter Kaye, a lingering interest in finding a way to do something meaningful was spurred to action by having lived through September 11th in Manhattan. We discussed that topic sometime in the year following as Peter worked to align his skills and values with a passion for making a difference in an early iteration of this exercise. He talks about the experience of finding that intersection as Vice President of Marketing at Honest Tea.

"Honest Tea brought a lot of it together," he says. "It was a consumer product and a beverage, but it truly had a mission-driven, consumer product difference. Those values that I had—bringing marketing, business, and beverage skills together with my values of trying to make a difference—checked just about all the boxes, so much so that I moved my family. We didn't really want to move, but it was one of those instances where I could genuinely say to my wife, 'This is the one.' It was a fabulous experience. It's exciting when you're having fun at what you're doing, leveraging your skills, and working in a place where you feel motivated and passionate. For me, it all came together at Honest Tea."

"Inside most people there is the desire to use their skills and align them with their passions," he continues. "Having worked in the organic industry for the last couple of years, talk about a bunch of people who are so passionate about what they do. It is about not compromising on what you stand for, how you make your product, and what you make it with. From my experience, the organic industry is a great example of folks who really are aligning passion with skills. Unfortunately, in my observation, there are a lot of people at big companies who either are there because they like to live in that market or they have strong family roots. They're punching the clock and they're doing a job. I didn't feel like Honest Tea was a job."

Peter's observations reflect what I've seen at Bolthouse Farms over the past few years. With CEO Jeff Dunn's goal of recasting the company at the forefront of the movement toward healthier eating, our culture and our workforce changed. Today, the passion people bring to the operation day in and day out energizes us all. We've become a place Millennials want to come and work because they want to be a part of our mission-centered objectives. It's been a phenomenal success story in terms of the financial side of the business, too, and all of that is about the alignment of our employees' personal passion with our mission.

FEEL YOUR PASSION.

If you still aren't sure what your passion is, if you aren't sure you have a passion, think about this. What makes your heart rate go up? What makes you talk faster, with more enthusiasm, and maybe a little bit louder? What puts you on your soapbox? What do you look forward to most? What could you lose yourself in for half a day without a second thought? Maybe there's no single answer to that question. If not, look more closely. Think about the answers to those questions. Then, look for the thread that connects them. You may have just found a way to define your passion—perhaps for motivating people, for creating impact, for inspiring change, for making your personal mark on the world.

> Complex people have a sparkle like a multi-faceted diamond that catches the eye and the interest of others.

Knowing your passion allows you to make it a part of what you do day in and day out. It allows you to find ways to incorporate it so that it becomes attached to your life and your success. Embracing and sharing your passion makes you more interesting. Complex people have a sparkle like a multi-faceted diamond that catches the eye and the interest of others.

My friend Rusty Rueff is a music guy. In college, he was a DJ and wanted more than anything to own a radio station. When he starts talking about music, there's an energy around him that you can't help but feel. It lights him up. Even when music wasn't part of his job, as Rusty built his career in human relations at PepsiCo and Electronic Arts, it was still part of what defined him. He used his love of music to connect with people, to be relatable, and to be really great at what he was doing. He's proof that when you know who you are, things come full circle. Today, he's a member of the Kennedy Center's Presidential Advisory Committee on the Arts, and Chairman Emeritus of The

Grammy Foundation, where he actively supports their Educator of the Year program. He is building a love of music in the next generation and sharing the love for his singular passion. Rusty stayed true to himself, sustained his passion even when it wasn't directly tied to his career, and today he's living it in ways he never dreamed of when we were in college.

PASSION SETS YOU APART.

In exploring values, we looked at the things in your life that matter to you. They represent a significant part of what defines you. But passion may be the place in which we find exactly what makes you special.

> Your most individually differentiating features are likely evidenced in the passion you bring to life.

Your passion, your enthusiasm, and your fire add color, add texture, add definition to who you are. Your most individually differentiating features are likely evidenced in the passion you bring to life. It is what makes you the most interesting to others, and as such may well drive your success, even if it does not directly tie to your career. Your passion will draw other passionate people to you. And you will all be enriched by that interaction.

There are many reasons those of us who hire want to know the passion of our potential employees. Regardless of whether your passion ties to your career, it is your indispensable fuel. Passion is what gets you across the finish line. It's what lands you on the podium. It's the inimitable secret sauce that fuels greatness. To Walmart founder Sam Walton, it was irreplaceable. "I think I overcame every single one of my personal shortcomings by the sheer passion I brought to my work," said Walton. "I don't know if you're born with this kind of passion, or if you can learn it. But I do know you need it."

And that brings us to the objective that's been beckoning in the distance since we started this exercise—the intersection of your skills, values, and passion. Having enumerated all three allows you to consider how you might align them. Don't be discouraged if at first they seem light years apart. It can take some imagination to reach that intersection. With some creative thought, you might find a combination you had not considered before. We'll dive into that part of the story shortly.

Regardless, know this. Don't hide your passion. Let it illuminate you in the world. It makes you more compelling, more engaging, more appealing. It is the thing that makes you unforgettable. We're all just people on the same planet. And when we interact in an authentic way, whether it is in the workplace or elsewhere, the genuine human connections we build make all of our lives richer, fuller, more exceptional, and so much more worthwhile. Being who you truly are will always be more interesting than who you might try to be.

Being who you truly are will always be more interesting than who you might try to be.

Know your passion. Live it.

LET YOUR PASSION LIGHT THE WAY.

Look Inside.

Hear It.

Be Unforgettable.

Reality check

ARE YOU SURE YOU'VE PUT YOUR ALL INTO IT?

Sometimes, clarity hurts.

Let your past inform your future.

Make sure the feedback is honest.

8
REALITY CHECK

"CONFRONT THE DARK PARTS OF YOURSELF, AND WORK
TO BANISH THEM WITH ILLUMINATION AND FORGIVENESS.
YOUR WILLINGNESS TO WRESTLE WITH YOUR DEMONS
WILL CAUSE YOUR ANGELS TO SING. USE THE PAIN AS FUEL,
AS A REMINDER OF YOUR STRENGTH."

August Wilson, Playwright

There you sit, the results of your hard work staring back at you. And let's be honest, you've done a ton of work. Goals... Skills... Values... Passion... About now, it feels like time for a break, doesn't it?

Well, breaks are overrated. Take a breath. Before you move forward, we need to have a conversation.

The work here is not for the faint-hearted. No one is denying that. It's deep, it's introspective, it's painful at times. Right? You are agreeing, aren't you? If not, you may need to take a harder look at what you've done so far. If it came together easily, if it was really no big deal, well, are you sure you put your all into it? Are you sure you found the right people to share this with? Take a moment to see how much truth is staring back at you from that piece of paper. The fact is, even if you worked your ass off, even if you were sweating blood over it, this is so hard that when you thought you were done, you might look closely and discover you still have much more work left to do.

Dave, my former colleague puts it this way. "When you first gave me the exercise, I totally underestimated how difficult it would be and how difficult I would make it on myself. On a high level, you think it shouldn't be difficult. But it is, if you really do it right."

It still surprises me sometimes, how hard it can be for people to identify their skills, values, and passion in a genuine way. It's often a hot mess the first couple of times people work through it. The SVP Exercise forces you to ask questions you don't like to ask. I get that. The exercise itself is not hard but the level of introspection required to apply it in a meaningful way is not an easy thing.

There's that. But there's also this. If you have done the work, if it hurt, if it still hurts, there's another conversation we should have.

It's okay.

Really.

I promise.

YOU AREN'T ALONE.

You may be staring at a piece of paper that feels so true, it hurts. When you look at it, you may wilt in the face of the truth starting back at you. If you are sitting there asking yourself how you've ended up where you are today and wondering what happened to the years, you aren't alone.

As she thought about her homework, Karen McCullough from the Purdue Research Foundation realized how much life, simple day-to-day life, had swallowed the time it took to reflect on herself and her goals.

"I grew up as the perfectionist. I worked for **The work here is not** the grades and I *always* got A's. This trend **for the faint-hearted.** continued through college/grad school.... The perfectionism (which was completely unsustainable) was always positively reinforced, so that's why it continued. Then my dad died, then I got married, then I had children— blah, blah, blah. The perfectionist, who made everyone happy all the time and did everything perfectly all the time, is no more. And life

My SVP homework

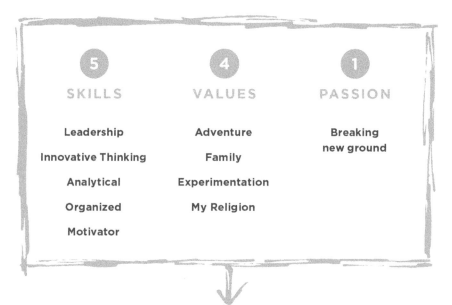

5	4	1
SKILLS	**VALUES**	**PASSION**
Leadership	Adventure	Breaking new ground
Innovative Thinking	Family	
Analytical	Experimentation	
Organized	My Religion	
Motivator		

MY STORY

I believe that just below the surface, there is
something extraordinary waiting to emerge.
Every person, every brand, and every
organization has an inspired future that few
can even imagine and even fewer ever pursue.
My unique role is to help organizations and
people envision their biggest future and provide
the clarity, focus, and courage to achieve it.

circumstances have kept me too busy to spend much time re-evaluating the person I have evolved into. Long story short: This is tough for me."

As he reflected on our SVP conversation, Jack told me, "You don't know it, but when you asked me what I really wanted to do with my life, it sent me spiraling down, skipping over the top of depression about where I was in my life." He went on to explain, "There's a vulnerability piece to it when you are asking these large questions about a person's passion and values. You're getting a window into somebody; it's very intimate. I realized, this is opening up a lot about me, going into my passion, my vulnerability, my strengths, my weaknesses. For a while, honestly, I felt embarrassed that I couldn't, at the time, articulate just the basics of what should be guiding my life."

There's no denying that sometimes, clarity hurts. Know this: You can't change the past, but you are not condemned to repeat it.

DON'T LOOK BACK.

You've identified your strengths and you've set tangible goals. Now is a time to look forward, informed by your past, not hamstrung by it. With a commitment to embracing your truth, the path forward will open up new opportunities and new adventures that will enrich your life. And when you control your path, I promise you, your confidence will grow like a muscle and will become stronger and stronger as you exercise it. With that, you will find yourself feeling good about the ways in which you are moving your life forward.

> With a commitment to embracing your truth,
> the path forward will open up new opportunities
> and new adventures that will enrich your life.

No one—no one—makes it through life without bumps along the way. So maybe you've just seen a bump you never even realized was there; it's okay. Remember this bit of wisdom from a pretty successful guy: "Making your mark on the world is hard. If it were easy, everybody would do it. But it's not. It takes patience, it takes commitment, and it comes with plenty of failure along the way. The real test is not whether you avoid this failure, because you won't. It's whether you let it harden or shame you into inaction, or whether you learn from it; whether you choose to persevere." Yup, that pearl of wisdom, complete with plenty of failure along the way, comes from President Barack Obama in a 2006 speech to the Campus Progress Annual Conference. He was talking about a vision for America, but it's a message that resonates at an individual level as well. For the President, perseverance led him to the White House and the opportunity to lead. Consider your goals, what you want out of life, and understand that half of getting there requires a commitment to not giving up even when the path is challenging.

For you, whether you realize you didn't push as hard on the SVP Exercise as you might have, or if the results of your homework left you with a black hole in the pit of your stomach, now is the time to commit to persevere.

So do this: Dig deeper. Revisit the entire process and ask yourself if the words on that piece of paper really reflect you, all of you, exactly as you would like to present yourself to the world. It may take weeks, or even a couple of months, of looking at this document and really thinking about it. You might even put it away for a bit so you can revisit it with fresh eyes. To reach the point where it's precisely what you want, consider what you've written down: Are those your most exceptional skills? Are they truly the values that guide you through life? Reread the Skills, Values, and Passion chapters of this book. You might see points you overlooked before you started your homework in earnest.

GET FEEDBACK FROM SOMEONE YOU TRUST.

Go back to a trusted friend or family member. Ask them to look again. Tell them to be brutally honest. They may be able to help you state your skills in a way that adds more clarity. They may call you out for presenting your values in a way that doesn't feel true to the person they know you to be. Remember, the goal isn't to earn a gold star on your homework. You want meaningful feedback, and then really, *really* think about it. You may look at your document and decide it was perfect, or you may spend more time refining it. Both outcomes are completely valid. There's no deadline, so take the time you need. Make it right, not quick.

Jack spent nearly a year on his homework before he felt ready to share it with others. "I was having a quasi-existential crisis, trying to understand: Who am I? What am I doing? What do I want to accomplish with my life? In the very beginning, the question, the homework, owned me a little bit. I'm very much about finding a structure, essentially a chart that I could map out. It owned me until I could piece it out as a flow chart of my life. I had all of the pieces out there. About three months later, I made some feeble attempts at putting the skills, values, passion down, and that's when I realized how feeble it was. It wasn't until months later that I felt like I had something that was sharp enough to share. I would have never predicted how much I had been floating and how much of myself I was leaving on the table," Jack says.

> Remember, the goal isn't to earn a gold star on your homework.

Reflecting back on the SVP Exercise and the long journey of working through his homework, he calls it eye-opening. "Through this, I've gotten a sense of confidence, a stronger self-awareness of who I am. That's helped me see things in a different light. I have a direction that I'm headed toward that feels good, and that's very empowering."

My friend Jessica also worked on this exercise for nearly three months to get it to the point of being ready to let anyone read it. Even though she thought it was complete at a couple of different points along the way, she continued to hold it close, kept staring at it, and put it away for a while. She noted at least three major revisions along the way before it felt like the story was complete as she really wanted to tell it. Then, after feedback from two close friends, Jessica examined it and changed it, twice more. "Finding the right words, and cutting through some notion of what I thought it *should be* to find what was true," she says, "was much more difficult than I realized." Completing the SVP Exercise also was a more emotional process than she had anticipated.

"There was a part of this that was energizing when it started. Taking the time to do something purposeful—something that was about me and not my kids and not my family—this was a new kind of experience for me," she explains. "But at the same time, as things first started to come into focus, as I thought about who I was, what I wanted to accomplish, what I hadn't yet accomplished... suddenly all I could see were all of these years that were irretrievably lost. There was so much time that I could never get back. For a while, that was paralyzing, really devastating. I couldn't finish the homework, and I couldn't focus on the idea of going forward. I couldn't imagine doing anything with it. At some point though, you just have to pick yourself up. You have to leave the past in the past. You can't put it anywhere else anyway. Then, finally, I was able to finish, to create this full picture that is incredibly empowering and that makes me very excited for what's next."

KEEP LOOKING FORWARD.

Don't forget Maxine Green and her notion of wide awakeness. That's not all sweetness and light. Her words are worth repeating here. "The only way to really awaken to life, awaken to the possibilities, is to be self-aware.... Consciousness doesn't come automatically; it comes through being alive, awake, curious, and often furious." To find yourself furious or even devastated is a genuine emotional reaction in the midst of becoming wide awake. Recognize that, accept it, deal with it, and move forward.

> To find yourself furious or even devastated is a genuine emotional reaction in the midst of becoming wide awake.

As you look back to what brought you to this place, don't forget the lessons of chaos theory. Have you heard of the butterfly effect? It's an element of chaos theory that argues that the smallest detail, as small as the motion of a butterfly's wings, can result in dramatic change over the course of time. Put more simply, all that you were defines all that you are. To change even a moment in your past might well change every subsequent moment. "Our lives are defined by opportunities, even the ones we miss," observed F. Scott Fitzgerald. That you are here today, reading this book, completing this work, comes from everything you were before. Your past is what got you here. Let it energize you and sustain you. Italian actress Sophia Loren once said, "There is a fountain of youth: It is your mind, your talents, the creativity you bring in your life and the lives of people you love." Let them keep you young.

Even as you complete the SVP Exercise, write your story, and formulate the plan that will take you to your next thing, don't forget to enjoy the journey. That you are making this effort is a great thing. Celebrate yourself and the goals you have already met through this exercise. Don't defer happiness as you pursue your dreams. Embrace it. Let your commitment to taking charge of your life embolden you.

Step into yourself. Savor every moment.

BE SURE YOU'VE LOOKED HARD ENOUGH TO FIND YOUR TRUTH.

Dig Deeper.
Take Charge.
Be Bold.

adding
it up

HOW WILL YOU KNOW WHEN IT'S RIGHT?

Does it feel comfortable?

Does it sound like you?

Does it energize and excite you as you start to tell it?

9
ADDING IT UP

"SO WRITE YOUR STORY AS IT NEEDS TO BE WRITTEN.
WRITE IT HONESTLY, AND TELL IT AS BEST YOU CAN.
I'M NOT SURE THAT THERE ARE ANY OTHER RULES.
NOT ONES THAT MATTER."

Neil Gaiman, Author

There it rests in front of you: The harvest of all your hard work. You've set a goal. You've looked inside, thought deeply, and compiled a list of your five exceptional skills, four core values, and one true passion. It's got to feel good. Getting to this point with the SVP Exercise requires a level of introspection and a hard, honest assessment that few of us are accustomed to amid the demands of daily life. You did it. Take a minute. You should feel really proud of what you've done.

This is a special point in the Exercise. The confidence I see in the face of someone whose homework is complete, the empowerment when the words are right—it's a cool thing. When you begin to build the momentum and when you get your legs under you, those are the signals that allow me to say, "Your homework is done. It's time to move ahead."

Let's talk about that next step. With the building blocks in front of you, it's time to pull it all together into the personal story that captures who you are and how (at this moment) you envision your place in the

SKILLS + VALUES + PASSION

world. Remember all of the gibberish and anxiety that the question "What do you want to be when you grow up?" caused earlier? Now, you have the tools to answer that question clearly and deliberately. You've forged a foundation to build upon and grow from as you move forward.

It's time to incorporate the elements of your homework into a simple story, your guiding belief. That will become your touchstone as you move toward your next thing, whether you use it in person, online, or in print.

IT'S ALL ABOUT STORYTELLING.

Think hard about this piece of homework in terms of telling your story. When I look at what's happening today in corporate marketing, I see a lot of focus on mission. A mission-centered organization becomes compelling when it tells its story. What it does comes into the world through the story it tells of the mission it aspires to fulfill. At Bolthouse Farms, our story is about much more than subsurface agriculture. It's about health and wellness. It's about eating better, living better, feeling better. For us, "Inspiring the Fresh Revolution" and "Making the Healthy Choice the Easy Choice" mean creating a better lifestyle for you and for your kids. Our story inspires the people who work at Bolthouse Farms. Even more,

> You should feel really proud of what you've done.

told well—at the right time, to the right audience—our story inspires our customers. It captures their attention and guides their actions as consumers. The momentum generated by living your mission attracts resources and creates opportunity in the corporate world. At a personal level, your objective (and your opportunity) is to craft your story in a way that garners attention and moves you forward, propelled by the momentum of the mission that drives you.

To create this three to five sentence paragraph is really not difficult work. Start with a summary statement that articulates what you believe. Add the specifics to explain it in more detail, and then conclude with a sentence that explains how you add value within that particular space.

In the early 1980s, *The Sunday Telegraph*, a British newspaper, introduced the concept of the mini saga with a writing contest. A mini saga is an uber short story, exactly 50 words in length: no more, no less. Conceptually, writing a mini saga forces you to be creative and to pare down the essential aspects of your story, all with the discipline of forced brevity. There's no 50-word requirement here, but the general goals of a mini saga reflect your objective. Think of your story as a mini saga, describing your special place in the world and your aspirations for your life.

There's no hard and fast formula, but consider a few examples that might help you capture the essence and rhythm of what you will write.

I believe that just below the surface, there is something extraordinary waiting to emerge. Every person, every brand, and every organization has an inspired future that few can ever imagine and even fewer ever pursue. My unique role is to help organizations and people envision their biggest future and provide the clarity, focus, and courage to achieve it.

The goal for my career is to always work in a communication/ marketing role that I am passionate about, one that will enable me to grow my skills without compromising any of my core values.

When we are willing to think differently, we can change things dramatically. *Meaningful solutions and creative change are in reach when we let go of doing the same things in the same ways and consider new solutions and new opportunities that open doors we never noticed existed. I make a difference by helping people see opportunities from new perspectives and consider solutions they had not imagined.*

As an aspiring designer with an affinity for classic design creatively rendered, I am committed to learning and innovation. I will bring my creative thinking, leadership, and problem solving skills to a team dedicated to devising inspiring consumer experiences.

We can change the world when we commit to making it better. *I believe in the power of words to convey complex ideas clearly, to interpret important data, and to be a catalyst for meaningful change in solving the world's most "wicked problems." All change begins with the story of what can be. That's the story I want to tell.*

Simple. Straightforward. Distinctive. Honest. Relevant. Relatable. Believable. Convincing. Clear. Memorable.

TELL THE STORY OF YOUR DIFFERENCE.

Write a paragraph that fulfills all of those criteria. And then, reread it for what matters most of all. Make sure that it feels authentic, that it represents what you think in a way that is real and true. Early in the process, I've heard people say the words can sound robotic and cold. If that's the case, you're probably still trying too hard to write what you think people want to hear and not what you want to say. Take a moment. Think about your story and how you would tell it sitting cross-legged on the floor with a friend. That's where you'll find the distinctive voice that is genuinely you. At the outset, we agreed that each of us possesses an array of qualities that defines our unique value, makes us different, better, special. There is no one who is exactly like you. Even if your twin walks the planet, there is still no one else who presents him or herself to the world precisely as you do. With this story, claim your special place in the world.

Expressing my place in the world was another lesson that became important for me at Procter & Gamble. There was a degree to which the group I was in, marketing, tended to be pretty homogenous. We were doing the same thing, working toward the same outcomes, vying for the same promotions, and approaching a lot of things the same way. The recognition of the overall sameness of me and my colleagues was an integral part of what taught me the importance of finding a way to stand out and being able to illustrate that. For me, that meant driving hard toward my most differentiating feature: Being a liberal arts major straight out of undergrad in a group of MBAs. Playing to my ability to think creatively and solve problems in a different way allowed me to separate myself from the people around me.

> With this story, claim your special place in the world.

This isn't unique to me or my situation at P&G. More often than not, we are swimming in a pool of people a lot like us. Being able to differentiate ourselves is crucial. Karen McCullough talks about that in the context of her early career as a singer and her brother's as a young actor in New York. "There are so many thirty-somethings out there trying to find 'meaningful work,'" she says. "This is why I told my brother, a white male actor, that his cleft lip is serving him well. He's memorable for it. It's why I used to wear bright stripes or polka dots to auditions. We all need to find a way to be distinctive. When we can't *wear* the distinction, we need to be able to *articulate* it."

STATE YOUR SKILLS CLEARLY.

Alongside the broad strokes that set you apart, take care to express your tangible skills as well. It's critical that you accurately and clearly say what you can do and know exactly what you have to offer. The 2014 Career Advisory Board (CAB) Job Preparedness Indicator Study by DeVry University found that only seven percent of hiring managers believed the majority of job applicants had the skills needed to meet the requirements of their open positions. In an article about the study in *Fast Company*, CAB Chair and vice president of student services at DeVry, Madeleine Slutsky, interpreted the results differently. "My prediction is that the skills are there—candidates just aren't conveying them effectively." Be aware of this as you think about how to best articulate your different, better, special value.

As you pull your SVP homework together and prepare to write, you should know that you will not include every word from that piece of paper in your personal story. Capture the spirit, the nuance of what's there, but that doesn't mean using every single bit. Think about your goals, and consider how your skills, values, and passion combine in support of those goals. Connecting the broad concepts is what matters here. That you know all of the elements of your homework and understand how they dovetail with your story is the most important takeaway. You will carry all those words in your backpack to be used as needed along the way as various situations arise.

Connecting the broad concepts is what matters here.

Consider the words of my former boss and Coca-Cola marketing executive Sergio Zyman as well: "Everything communicates." It's true. Everything you say, everything you don't say, speaks volumes. Whether it's in how you write this piece of homework or how you choose to use it moving forward, *Everything communicates*. Never forget that. Always be engaged in the conversation. It's your story. Control the dialogue and present it as you want it to be told. No less a business icon than Peter Drucker, the godfather of management theory, said, "The most important thing in communication is to hear what isn't being said." As you write, and as you present yourself to the world, keep that in mind. *Everything communicates*. Always.

WHEN IT'S RIGHT, YOU CAN FEEL IT.

Once you have your finished story, it should feel perfectly comfortable to you. It should roll easily off your tongue. Think of it as your personal elevator pitch. It should be the story you can tell without thinking about it, the story that energizes and excites you as you start to tell it. If your passion is in there, you'll feel it. It should be natural and come easily to you. Completed successfully, it's the story you would fall back to and embrace if you found yourself on stage addressing a theatre full of your peers.

Always be engaged in the conversation. It's your story

There's something I've seen repeatedly among the people who have found an extraordinary intersection of their skills, values, and passion. When you hear them tell their story, it feels unintentional. Their story is so perfectly put together, so clear, so pristine. It is an extension of their being and works effortlessly. It just *is*.

Now with your story, do this. Read it aloud. Really. Do it. Does it make you stumble? Are you comfortable with both the words you've chosen and the larger message? Does it sound like you? If not, the message might be there, but the words might still be off. Think about how you talk. Write with a level of formality or informality that feels like your usual cadence. It will help make the story truly yours. When it's done, it will be the soapbox you naturally step onto to talk about your place in the world and the specific difference that you alone can make.

ONCE AGAIN, SHARE IT.

At this point, it's time again to share your work with three to four close friends or family members. Always remember, the goal here is to get honest feedback. Ask them to push, not to just be nice or enable you. The point is to really tear it apart as a way to find your true voice and your special niche. Have them look back at the component pieces as well as your personal story.

An early conversation that evolved into the SVP Exercise occurred when Jeff Crow was still at Coca-Cola. He remembers, "Passion and what makes you different, those were the two foundations coming out of that initial review. What is it that you want to do? The reflex answer to that is usually a brand manager, a GM, a vice president. There's never enough texture there." It was in the subsequent conversations, as part of the feedback process, that Jeff found the dimensionality that is so crucial. "The great thing is, when you are having that conversation with someone who knows you well and isn't afraid to call BS, you end up in some really neat, really unexpected places. You say, 'I'm good at A, B, C, D,' and the response is, 'Yep, I see A and B, but I'm not so sure about C and D. I think that's something a little different.' That's what gets you somewhere interesting."

For Dave, the prospect of feedback meant setting a high bar for himself. "Going through the process, and knowing that there would be feedback, made me think a lot about what I was putting down. If I put the words on that page, I needed to be able to own it, to back it up, and feel strongly about it."

To reiterate my earlier point about writing it down, the important thing is to start getting words on paper. Don't be overly critical. Don't hold back. Just write. You'll revisit your words later and eventually share them with others. But you won't do anything productive until what's in your head makes it on paper and challenges you to find your truth. I said from the start, this process is messy. Embrace the mess. Get started.

> But you won't do anything productive
> until what's in your head makes it on paper
> and challenges you to find your truth.

Seriously though, it is a big thing. It's you. It's your life. You are worth the effort and worth the mess. As you gather your thoughts, you collect the range of broad ideas that you will assess, edit, and contemplate as you move through the process. It starts with you. Don't self-edit before you begin to put your words on a page. A little spit-balling, as I like to call it, is a terrific place to start.

So drink it all in. As you work through the next stage of writing and begin to clarify your thinking, seek input. Ask for feedback from people who know you well and care enough to tell you when you're wrong. The pieces they agree with and those they don't will all help clarify your thinking. Legendary basketball coach John Wooden once said, "Whatever you do in life, surround yourself with smart people who'll argue with you." That's not to suggest that you will be laying for a fight here. At the same time, you are better served by people who are willing to tell you "No" than those who always say "Yes."

The feedback of people who care enough about you to say "No, that's not how I see you," is invaluable. There's no one whose insight matters more in this process. Unvarnished truth from people you trust will make you think. It will make you question. It will make you see. You will take their feedback and find that you can still look harder than you have so far. Then, put everything through the "nobody cares" filter. Recognize that ultimately only you can truly say what you want. You must assess every bit of well-intentioned feedback to know what it really means to you. You may decide that they are right, or you may find yourself able to identify exactly why they are dead wrong. Either outcome is a terrific step forward. Armed with the input of people who know you well, you can find a level of truth that is so much harder to find on your own.

THE PROMISE OF NO.

When it hurts to hear "No, that's not what I see as your strength," think of it this way. "No" isn't a rejection of what you've done. It's a promise of belief in how much more you are capable of doing. It represents the gift of seeing yourself through someone else's eyes. When you find people who make you stretch and grow, consider yourself lucky. They believe in you and your potential. Hold onto them with both hands. The number of people you encounter in life who will positively challenge you is small. Appreciate them and tell them often.

With that feedback, look at all of your homework again. Consider the tweaks, or outright changes, suggested by your circle of family and friends. Ask yourself again: "Does it feel right?" Trust your gut. Often, it knows much more than you give it credit for. With a strong, credible story that communicates your truth, you can start the process of figuring out how to move forward with intent, toward your next thing in life.

You've done the work. Prepare to work the plan.

CREATE A STRONG, CREDIBLE STORY AND THINK ABOUT MORE.

Be Authentic.

Be Emotive.

Be Memorable.

applying SvP

HOW DO YOU PUT TOGETHER A PLAN?

Do your research.

Think about what you want to do.

Know your network and invoke it with intent.

10
APPLYING SVP

"TO ACHIEVE SUCCESS, WHATEVER THE JOB WE HAVE,
WE MUST PAY A PRICE FOR SUCCESS. IT'S LIKE ANYTHING
WORTHWHILE. IT HAS A PRICE. YOU HAVE TO PAY THE
PRICE TO WIN, YOU HAVE TO PAY THE PRICE TO GET
TO THE POINT WHERE SUCCESS IS POSSIBLE."

Vince Lombardi, Football Coach

You've worked it, and you've worked it again. You've shared that story in front of you with family and friends and received feedback that challenged you and maybe even lifted you up. It might be a little bit tough to wipe the smile off your face. When it's right, when the story you've written really captures what you care about, who you are, and where you're going, the sense of accomplishment is palpable. Now, it's time to take the next step.

All of the work you have done means nothing until you apply it. That may take the form of making bold changes or gaining more control and clarity about your place in the world. Again, the words are critical, but the actions that follow them enable you to *Be More*.

For Karen McCullough, her homework didn't point to sweeping changes. "I recognized that my old job wasn't it for me. I did the SVP Exercise, learned a lot, and took active steps to expand my network and find something that fit me better. To me, that is success. Circumstances may not be such that you can chuck it all, and move across the country. But that's okay! Nominal changes—that sense of empowerment—these make all the difference and poise you for bigger and better things down the line."

TIME TO MAKE YOUR PLAN.

At this point, it's time to assess your outcomes, create your plan for moving forward, and set it in motion.

When your plan includes a call for dramatic change, it's time to think hard about what that means and how to move toward the change you now envision in your life. I've seen people work the plan in many different ways. For one, that meant creating detailed spreadsheets with multiple columns weighing the relative merits of companies he wanted to assess as part of tracking his options. Others operate within different structures. It's all about how you think and how you work. At some level, how you attack the next stage of the process offers yet another reflection of you. It may be a multi-columned, multi-tabbed Excel spreadsheet. It may be a piece of notebook paper with a hand-drawn matrix scratched on it.

All of the work you have done means nothing until you apply it.

Look around and be highly aware of the people and events around you and how you perceive and are perceived. *Observe everything.* Understand how people view you, how that connects with the story you've created, and think about how to communicate what you have to offer. There may be a disconnect between how people view you right now and how you want to present yourself. Understanding how the perceptions of you that exist today relate to the story you are now prepared to tell will allow you to fill the gap in a manner designed to move you toward more.

As we have discussed, *everything communicates.* Consider how your skills, values, and passion intersect and how that directs your

RESEARCH

JOBS | COMPANIES | ORGANIZATIONS

COMMUNICATION TOOLS

RESUME | SOCIAL MEDIA

EXPLORE CONNECTIONS

PEOPLE WHO CAN GET YOU INTO THOSE PLACES

LEVERAGE NETWORK

"ASK EASY"

next thing. Think about where the goal you set points you and how the work you've done guides that. You've identified a series of guideposts to begin the next phase of your journey. Now it's time to figure out how to position your story—online, offline, and in your personal interactions—to advance your plan.

EXERCISE YOUR RESOURCES.

Do your research. Today, the ease with which we can learn more about organizations, their culture, and the opportunities inside them is unparalleled. Corporate websites provide a great first look into how they choose to present themselves. At the same time, take advantage of all that you can learn from sites like LinkedIn and Glassdoor to work toward gaining a broader perspective of the organizations you are researching.

✳ As you look at organizations, map their values alongside what you wrote. Consider fit and how well each organization aligns with what matters to you.

Now that you have a better awareness of yourself, you can determine the fit that makes sense for you. Look at the mission and value statements of companies and organizations that interest you. See how they mesh with what matters to you. If you've been really clear on your personal story, you will begin to see how you align with places that you target for your next thing. Then, when you get in the door, you'll be able to test in person to see if what you've read in advance matches what you learn from the people and even from the room itself.

Peter Kaye, one of the master spreadsheet builders in approaching his homework, continues to use the parameters of understanding his skills, and particularly his passion, as guideposts in considering career opportunities. He explains, "I evaluate on basic stuff: Do I like my boss, the compensation, the equity. But then overlaying it all is the question: 'How psyched will I be about this?' Using that filter allowed me... as I was interviewed and as I turned things around on those folks who had been interviewing me... to really dig beneath things by pushing around these things about mission and purpose. It was telling to me when I talked to multiple people in an organization, was it consistent or not?"

Read job descriptions on company websites, even for positions that don't interest you. The qualities a company chooses to highlight across the organization are relevant. They speak to what matters within their corporate culture. A friend talks about a position as president of a private family foundation that noted a sense of humor as a key characteristic of their ideal leader. While she didn't ultimately apply for the job, it's still memorable and reflects positively on the organization for her. The fact that they made the choice to include that trait in the job description for their president said a lot about the kind of work culture its founders valued.

FIT IS CRITICAL.

The importance of fit within a workplace culture can't be overstated. To reiterate, I would estimate that half of the people who are fired aren't fired because of a lack of skills but because of a poor fit. I believe using the SVP Exercise can help you avoid that. I talked about my experience at Princess Cruises. Personal disaster. Career disaster. That was all about poor fit. It was not the right place for me at all. It's also a job I stepped into without using SVP as a guide. That experience is part of what reinforced, for me, the importance of moving with intent. It's a two-way street. By working proactively, you can save yourself, and potential employers, time and money by having a clearer understanding of yourself and where you fit in. It's a win-win.

As you begin to develop a plan in terms of where you want to work, drill in further to consider what you want to do. Look at job postings and organizational contact lists to assess the different functions within your target companies and organizations. This will not only open your eyes to positions within the organizations that interest you, it may also broaden your understanding of the breadth of opportunities available across the spectrum. Through all of this, use the work you have done with the SVP Exercise as the lens through which you view your options. Be aware of job titles and job description keywords. Looking for overlap with elements of your personal document may make sense.

The importance of fit within a workplace culture can't be overstated.

NEXT TURN TO YOUR NETWORK.

Once you have identified target organizations and aspirational jobs, it's time to examine how that interfaces with your existing network. Here is another place where it may make sense to build a spreadsheet to more easily find your best strategy for moving toward your next thing. Note the companies that interest you and begin the process of determining who you know that either works there or has worked there. In many instances, people maintain connections with their former employers. Take a comprehensive look at where your contacts have been over the course of their careers.

Even connecting with people you don't know but who work in a field that interests you may be useful. Before she was hired for her first development job at the University of Pennsylvania, Karen McCullough reached out to people there asking for informational interviews. "I said, 'Here's who I am. I have a sincere interest in your organization. I'd love to hear more about what you do. Would you be willing to meet me for a quick cup of coffee?' I was shocked at how many people—high up people —met with me. On my first day working there, I saw a lot of friendly (and familiar) faces."

> ✳ You can only ask for help a limited number of times, so make certain you are ready and have a clear understanding of your potential resources.

Keeping with that theme, look at the fields in which people you know work. It's a small world, sometimes a teeny, tiny one. You will be amazed by the number of people across any given industry, public or private, for-profit or not-for-profit, who know one another. This should be built into your points of connection. Where you went to college also matters. Alumni networks can be enormously powerful. Speaking to a class at our shared alma mater, Lalita Amos tried to explain the importance of the Purdue network to students. "We love you," she said, "and we don't even know you yet." That's a pretty powerful statement of connection.

People with whom you share a commonality of experience, such as college, are often more than willing to have a conversation, meet for coffee, perhaps even make an introduction.

FINISH YOUR WORK FIRST.

Before you begin the process of actually reaching out though, be ready. Don't go too early. Begin by applying the relevant elements of your story to the many tactics available to you. Your story should be reflected in your résumé, your LinkedIn profile, your blog, and elsewhere. It should inform how you present yourself to your network. Remember when we talked about how you present yourself through your social media networks?

> **Your story should be reflected in your résumé, your LinkedIn profile, your blog, and elsewhere.**

Think purposefully about how you interact in that space. And don't discount its importance. For many people, LinkedIn and social media in general are a key talent resource. Whether looking at individuals they know or sharing their hiring needs across their network, it's often an important point of first contact. Being connected in your industry via social media is a way to be seen.

That audience can have a big impact on your career, so craft that part of your story with care and be well-positioned to move forward. But how do you know when you're ready? Readiness is something that can be really hard to assess. Ask other people to comment upon how you are positioning yourself before you take your show on the road with your network.

But what does that all really mean?

Review your résumé and online presence to determine how they can better reflect the skills you've identified. Consider the accomplishments you highlight and how they mesh with the story you've written. The key is to achieve a relevant and clear integration of what you've learned as a result of your homework and apply it to the documents, written and electronic, that represent you in the world. Your story should be concise, clear, compelling, and always, always consistent.

When you are ready to begin reaching out to your network, *ask smart*. Be certain you are using the lessons you learned through the SVP Exercise and are connecting the dots in a way that directs you to the right things. Don't use your connections too early, in the wrong way, or for the wrong things. Your network isn't a bottomless well. You probably get no more than three chances with any one individual. Too many requests, too many failed attempts, and you're going to look like a risk. People won't stake their reputations on someone who repeatedly, but unsuccessfully, reaches out for help. When you ask, make sure it counts. And if you do ask for a connection, please—please—follow up.

> **Your story should be concise, clear, compelling, and always, always consistent.**

KNOW WHAT YOU NEED.

And when you ask for help from your network, *ask easy*. Be concise. Be straightforward. Ask for exactly what you want. Don't beat around the bush. Do you want an introduction, a letter of recommendation, a résumé review, a reference? Say what you want. People don't want to waste their time figuring out what you need. If you ask for more than one thing in an email, number your requests. It becomes immediately easier to make a response. Need a letter sent? Provide the appropriate contact information and the details of the position for which you are applying. It may make sense to simply include it in the email. Nobody wants to do the work of looking through multiple website links. Determine what is relevant and put it in one place. Really want to get something done? When possible, copy your email request to the person's assistant.

Speaking of assistants, whether you are connecting with individuals in your network or potential employers, do not underestimate the value of your relationship with their assistants. Your ability to get in the door is often in their hands. Be polite. Be gracious. Be respectful. You may find yourself in a position to talk with them multiple times. Learn their names. It can be just as important to be liked and respected by an administrative assistant as anyone you encounter. The way that you treat people across the organization is a reflection on you and one that will be communicated and noticed.

People don't want to waste their time figuring out what you need.

None of this is rocket science. If you've done your research, connecting the dots will be easy, and moving toward your goals will become a clear process.

Observe everything. Everything communicates. Ask smart. Ask easy. Create your plan. Put it in motion.

APPLY WHAT YOU'VE LEARNED AND WORK YOUR PLAN.

Be Strategic.
Be Ready.
Be Respectful.

everything changes

WHEN DOES THE HOMEWORK END?

Revisit periodically and know the ways you are growing.

Update your narrative to move forward purposefully.

Be proactive, stay in control... it never ends.

11
EVERYTHING CHANGES

"OBSERVE CONSTANTLY THAT ALL THINGS TAKE PLACE
BY CHANGE, AND ACCUSTOM THYSELF TO CONSIDER
THAT THE NATURE OF THE UNIVERSE LOVES NOTHING
SO MUCH AS TO CHANGE THE THINGS WHICH ARE,
AND TO MAKE NEW THINGS LIKE THEM."

Marcus Aurelius

There it is. The fruits of your labor are beginning to take shape. You've taken a really hard look at yourself, your life, what you're great at, and what really matters to you. You've set a goal, and cataloged your skills, values, and passion. You are able to talk about your unique value, your personal mission, and what reaching toward more looks like for you.

It's all right to kick back, put your feet up—bonbons and lollipops for everyone. You're in charge. You're owning it, and it feels good.

You know where you're going, and your next thing will be a better fit, and your life will feel better as a result.

But don't give this book away to a friend. There will be a time when you turn to it again. Life happens, people change, and even your dream job may not always hold the same allure.

WHAT WAS PERFECT BEFORE MAY NOT BE TODAY.

What does that mean? Are we unable to recognize what we want? Of course not. People change, organizations change, family situations change. Any number of factors can transform a dream job into something less than dreamy.

My friend Jessica talks about the two dream jobs she has held within her organization and reflects on them as a result of working through the SVP Exercise. In the first, she described it as the perfect, unexpected culmination of all her education and prior work experience. That said; she was the first to admit that serendipity, not careful career planning, landed her there. But sometime during her seventh year, she realized that she had grown beyond the job. She was thrilled with what she had accomplished, but the foundation was in place for someone else to step in. She needed a new challenge. The job felt too small.

Life happens, people change, and even your dream job may not always hold the same allure.

Her next position, a more purposeful career step, grew into that same perfect place with a tight-knit, collegial team. She had the opportunity to make a big impact, and a meaningful mission. Until, one day, it became more frustrating than rewarding. Jessica explains, "For weeks, I drove into work with tears in my eyes. It was so hard to figure out why this job I had loved too much to leave had become draining. The job hadn't changed, so I knew that I had. But what I ultimately realized is that it had become my bad boyfriend. I was more invested in it and in moving the organization forward than the organization was. Carrying it on my back, pouring my heart into it with little recognition of the important steps we were making, snuffed out what had made it, for a while, my dream job."

RESPOND TO THE CHANGES IN YOUR LIFE.

When that happens, it's time to reassess. Everything we have talked about changes. Over the course of your life, different goals will excite you at different points in time. Your skills will grow and become more refined, and your ability to harness them will provide the flexibility to take you in new directions. As you grow and develop, it makes sense that your career should as well. If that stops, it may be time to revisit your plan, understand what in and around you has changed, and take back control in a proactive way.

Everything we have talked about changes.

When I went to work at Coca-Cola, it was a perfect place for me. The balance of analytical and creative skills I brought to the table was a great fit there. Alongside Procter & Gamble, it's a place where I learned a lot, a place that really shaped me. But after I'd been there a few years, I began to question the value of what we were doing. I knew we weren't helping the world as much as CEO Doug Daft thought we were. At the same time, my wife, Rachel, who had grown up on the West Coast, wanted to go back there. So those two values pieces, my perception of the place of my work in the world and a family dynamic, resulted in the decision to leave the company. As I said earlier, careers don't exist in a vacuum. They need to work in concert with our lives and all of the complexity and nuance that are a part of them. The better handle you have on what all of those moving pieces mean in your life, the better equipped you are to make decisions that are good for you.

BE ATTUNED TO YOUR PLACE IN THE WORLD.

Whatever the reason, when it's time for a change, do it with intent. The homework you've completed as part of the SVP Exercise, performance reviews from work, accolades and negative feedback you've received along the way—all of it helps you to chart your journey. File them all away. All of these things combine to create a mosaic of your career trajectory. You may need to step back to see the picture more clearly, but gathered together, these items enable you to reflect on your personal evolution, to see how you have changed and grown through the years, and to understand what influences along the way have shaped you.

As the time comes to set new goals and refine your plan, having this narrative will help you move forward in a more deliberate manner.

Eric Johnson, my colleague from Coca-Cola, regularly pulls out his homework to assess where he is. "The biggest thing for me is to continue going back to these essential truths and saying, 'Are you living up to these things?' For me that's been a bit of a routine, I look at that every month. I take a deep dive every year between Christmas and New Year's. I kind of go off into the woods to really think. I challenge myself all the time to see if I'm being true to my plan."

> All of these things combine to create a mosaic of your career trajectory.

That even led him to a career change. "I've always been part of a giant company," Eric notes, "but I wanted to do something more entrepreneurial. That led me to the Snyder's of Hanover people and the pretzel business. It's a much smaller organization, a much different context.... There have been times, I wondered if I could really push, if they would understand what I'm trying to do. But I go back to that list and think about why I'm here. The reality is they need the things I can do just as much as Kraft or Coke needed them."

With this exercise, you've captured a moment in time, but your life is not carved in stone, not while you are still breathing. Look back at what you wrote. Think about how you would have written the same document five years ago, or ten. It would look considerably different in many ways. The same will be true five, ten, twenty years from now. While your core values may not change, the articulation of them will change over time. What it means to value family will be tied to very different demands at different points in your life. We also know ourselves differently at different stops along the way. Your desire to make an impact in the world will mean something very different at different points of your life.

"Everything does change," agrees Jeff Crow. "When you have a wife and a family and a mortgage, it shakes your perspective. You feel more vulnerable and less invincible. Using the language from Coke, it's made me more of a camper and less of a climber. To me, it is all about my family and supporting my family and having the flexibility to be with them." Alongside changes in life situation and responsibility, he points to the sheer passage of time as well. "I think of myself as a young guy, but I'm not one of the young kids at work anymore. There are more people younger than me than older than me. There are more people who look to me than I look toward. Everything does change, and with a lot of things, you probably can't control them."

"I've had some particularly memorable experiences, from a learning standpoint, experiences I draw upon," says Peter Kaye. "Early in my career, I was at Nestle in the candy business, my six years at Coke was a great learning experience, Diageo gave me international experience. But with all three of them I absolutely had moments where I had to ask myself, 'Where's the meaning in this?' Getting people to drink more soft drinks, eat more candy, to have another vodka and soda... getting people to have more of this was just not fulfilling. Had I found something else, I might have moved to something more purpose driven sooner. I probably had kind of a percolating desire within me to do something making a difference. I think 9/11 was a big trigger to say yeah, I really want to do that. It may take a bit to get there. But that's what I want."

> Your desire to make an impact in the world
> will mean something very different
> at different points of your life.

Over time, passions, too, can evolve. Your love of mountain climbing in your twenties may morph into a love of biking in another decade or two. The constant may be your love of the outdoors, but the way in which you experience it, and the places you want it to take you, can point you in new directions.

Embrace the changes that will allow you to live a life that is true to what matters the most to you. "Your work is going to fill a large part of your life, and the only way to be truly satisfied is to do what you believe is great work," Steve Jobs reminds us. "And the only way to do great work is to love what you do. If you haven't found it yet, keep looking. Don't settle." Hold on to the commitment you are making today to stay fierce, stay restless, as you move purposefully forward in your life.

Now, you have the tools that will allow you to pivot at any point. You have in your hands a snapshot in time. When you need to, you are prepared to take another snapshot, to reassess as you move forward with intent. You have a tool, the SVP Exercise, and you know how to use it. If you are fully present in your life, if you remain wide awake, you will recognize when the time comes to

Embrace the changes that will allow you to live a life that is true to what matters the most to you.

turn your thoughts deeply inside once again. Then, you can take your homework out of your backpack, maybe open this book once again, and update your story to match your life.

Everything changes. Own your change.

EMBRACE CHANGE WITH THE LESSONS YOU HAVE LEARNED.

Be Aware.

Look Inside.

Stay True.

what's
next?

HOW WILL YOU KNOW WHEN IT'S RIGHT?

Does it feel comfortable?

Does it sound like you?

Does it energize and excite you as you start to tell it?

12
WHAT'S NEXT?

"TWENTY YEARS FROM NOW YOU WILL BE MORE DISAPPOINTED
BY THE THINGS YOU DIDN'T DO THAN BY THE ONES YOU DID.
SO THROW OFF THE BOWLINES. SAIL AWAY FROM THE
SAFE HARBOR. CATCH THE TRADE WINDS IN YOUR SAILS.
EXPLORE. DREAM. DISCOVER."

Mark Twain, Author and Humorist *(attributed)*

It's been quite a ride, hasn't it? Even if you read the book quickly, even if you haven't really taken a deep dive into your homework yet, it's gotten into your head.

What do you want to be when you grow up?

You really can't make the question go away, can you? Man, I sure hope not.

When what you want is more, just more, being able to answer that question goes a long way toward getting you there.

That simple question really gets people into a twist, maybe because it seems too big, too daunting. It seems like an end game. To answer it seems overwhelmingly definitive. Once you've answered it, and once you've accomplished it, what's next? What else is there? Are you done? I don't see it that way at all. "What do you want to be when you grow up?" is just another metric. It's just another moving goal that you slide forward as you progress through life. It's another piece of your story that changes as you change. Answering it isn't final. Answering it gives life and depth and energy to you and to your story. Answer it today. Pursue that aspiration. Attain it and set your sights on what's next.

As I said at the outset, I wanted to write this book for a long time. I wanted to write it because it makes me crazy when people—really smart, accomplished people—can't answer that question. It makes me crazy when people are willing to just coast through life, maybe because they're afraid to challenge the status quo, maybe because they don't want to risk failing, or maybe because they simply don't know how to get started. No more excuses. Now, you have a way to get started.

No more excuses. Now, you have a way to get started.

I wanted to write this book to see the enlightenment on people's faces, to see the recognition that their capacity for growth and achievement outweighs their greatest fears, and to help them see that more is absolutely within reach. For me, leading people—galvanizing people to do more, perhaps more than even they believe they can do—is my true passion. At its core, it's cool to see people succeed in a way that they define, to control their own destiny rather than leave it in the hands of someone else or some cold organization, and to move toward more in a way that is meaningful to them.

HOW WILL YOU MOVE TOWARD MORE?

Now, as you near the moment of putting this book down, I know that in your mind, the wheels are turning faster. You are thinking about your goals, defining who you are and where you want to go. You're thinking about what you do well and acknowledging those things you don't do so well. You're thinking about what matters most to you, what makes life, for you, indescribably worth living. Because now you can see it's about the difference you want to make in the world and how you will design that mission.

Momentum is good. Getting going is progress. Stimulating the conversation in your head and envisioning a more directed path seems to give people the confidence they need to move forward. Having come this far together, my hope is that in *Be More*, and with the Skills Values Passion Exercise, you've found a straightforward way to bring more control to your crazy life and to channel your energies toward what you want. As it took shape through the years, my objective was for the SVP Exercise to become a simple, practical guide to help people better understand their unique gifts and their personal mission—and to put those in a context that feels empowering and allows them to express their story in a relevant, relatable way.

Momentum is good. Getting going is progress.

If your homework is still a work in progress, keep plugging away. You'll get through the exercise if you stick with it. Think about it, ask questions, consider every bit of feedback you receive. One day, the pieces will come together in the space of a moment, and you won't even remember when you couldn't say what suddenly comes to you as naturally as breathing. I've seen it happen time and again. You'll pause and recognize that you are carrying yourself with more confidence than before. Alongside that, you will be aware of something else, something quieter. You will experience a sense of balance that comes from knowing yourself. When the words are right, when you achieve clarity, when you say who you are and what you want, you don't just voice it: You feel it. Your confidence and self-awareness will sustain you, regardless of what life might throw your way.

WHEN YOU KNOW YOURSELF, YOU OWN YOUR DESTINY.

With that knowledge, you'll be armed to move forward with intent in the way that you define. That could mean a small tweak in career direction, a hard left turn toward a completely new thing, or the realization that you can get even more out of a current job that is already a pretty good fit. Once you can define your SVP and articulate your story, you will have a better understanding of what it means to you to *Be More*. Regardless of which outcome you choose, that's the critical part—you choose. It's your next thing, and you own it. As you take your next step, even when it's scary, the fear of the unknown will be offset by the understanding that your decisions are yours, and by the strength that comes from knowing what matters most to you and why.

As you move toward implementing your plan for what's next, hold fast to the other lessons you've learned. Be highly aware of the world around you. Observe everything. Never forget, as Sergio Zyman said so many times: Everything communicates. Present your truest self to the world. Find energy in the knowledge that there are no carbon copies on the planet. Each of us is different, better, special, with the capacity to be more, and each brings an undeniably differentiated set of experiences, perspectives, and skills to all that we touch. There is no one who can replicate you—let that be your rallying cry to celebrate your most authentic self as your greatest asset. With that in mind, plan your strategy and chart your course. Leverage your connections as you align yourself with organizations that are a fit for you. Ask smart. Ask easy. Ask at the right time. There's a lot more out there.

> It's your next thing, and you own it.

Nelson Mandela once said, "There is no passion to be found in playing small—in settling for a life that is less than you are capable of living."

It's that life, the one you are capable of living, the life that will be meaningful and fulfilling to you, that you will be empowered to pursue. That's what I want you to take away from this book.

REACH FOR ALL YOU CAN BE.

With a vision for what you want and a plan for how you will get there, I expect you to be energized about the future that awaits. With a clear vision of your skills, values, passion, it will be easier to see in a very obvious way the progress you are making toward achieving your goals. To control your destiny, to define your path, and to chart your progress will allow you to better understand, and celebrate, the difference you make in the world. With clearly-defined goals, you will also be more attuned to your clearly-defined wins.

Based on my experience, my expectation is that this book will be revisited again and again. Return to your SVP Exercise on a regular basis. Whether you schedule it at the end of the year as I do, or perhaps as each birthday arrives, come back to it at least annually. Update your skills, add your performance reviews to the file where you keep it. The document should be a living, breathing thing, just as you are. All of us change, learn, grow every day. You keep moving and evolving, and your SVP homework should as well. Keeping it current keeps it relevant. That's how it can serve you best.

Then, when new opportunities arise, whether they are for new jobs, projects, or business prospects, let the hard work you have put into your homework be the rudder that allows you to drive decision making on terms that serve your larger goals. Reference your SVP Exercise to measure your progress over time or to help you reroute your course when that makes sense. When the time comes and once again, you find yourself longing for more, remember you have created this touchstone that can help you assess and move forward. Leverage it to your full benefit. With an eye to the longer term, as time passes, you will be able to review past SVP Exercises to see the arc of your career more easily and you will be able to make adjustments along the way that allow you to move toward your goals in the way that you define.

With clearly-defined goals, you will also be more attuned to your clearly-defined wins.

Almost from the first discussion about *Be More*, there's been an unending tug-of-war between the notion of this book as a practical guide and the aspiration of the outcomes it intends to affect. Having worked through the SVP Exercise and having found a greater margin of control in your life, I hope you will find yourself more content, and that you will enjoy a greater measure of happiness. Being happier in life may be the single thing to which we all aspire. That said, while happiness may in fact be a byproduct of this book, it's not the end goal I had in mind in the beginning.

USE THIS AS A PRACTICAL TOOL.

For me, success means that you talk about the book, and about the SVP Exercise in particular, as a practical tool to find your truth, to learn to tell your story, and to empower you to direct momentum to get what you want. History teaches us, it takes something practical to achieve something extraordinary. Every great aspiration is achieved through a series of actions that, when pared down to their bare essence, represent nothing more exotic than simple, practical, hard work.

While writing this book, I said that I didn't expect to change the whole world in one broad stroke. I wanted it to reach one person at a time, to help individuals at a personal level. I hope this book speaks to you that way. My intent for the SVP Exercise has always been for it to function as an effective, versatile tool. As with any good tool, I hope it makes the work easier and will be well-used through the years. Perhaps you will even loan it to your neighbor on occasion.

To that end, as you move your life forward, I want you to do this. Share what you've learned. Pay it forward. Talk with your friends and coworkers about their goals. Help them recognize their skills, values, and passion, all of which makes them undeniably unique. Help them say what getting more out of life really means to them. Raise your children to take control of their destinies. Talk about accountability and responsibility. Teach your kids about preparation, or as Rusty likes to say, "To lay your clothes out the night before." It's never too early to start. If you asked my mom, she'd tell you I was setting annual goals when I was a youngster. There's no reason not to begin that at an early age. How cool would it be to see a generation with more kids developing ideas of what they want to be when they grow up?

History teaches us, it takes something practical to achieve something extraordinary.

SHARE THE LESSONS YOU LEARNED.

Maybe that's my one true aspiration for this book: That you will share its lesson with someone, who will share its lesson with someone, who will share its lesson with someone. Maybe my ultimate wish is that it will resonate with you in a way that makes it reverberate among more people than I can reach all by myself. Maybe my wish is that the straightforward, practical SVP Exercise, paired with the recognition that we all simply want more, and need to be able to tell the story of what that means to us, will take on a life of its own.

> *Great* is something we all have the capacity to be once we can outline our mission and understand where our capability for impact lies.

I believe that working toward something beyond our reach is what we are programmed to do. It's in our DNA. It's why we explore. It's why we discover. It's why we ask *why*. The siren song of the unknown, the yet-to-be-experienced, that's what inspires innovation, creativity, progress. That's what makes good *great*. And *great* is something we all have the capacity to be once we can outline our mission and understand where our capability for impact lies.

Looking ahead, do this: Dare to do more. Move forward emboldened by the vision of what you want to be when you grow up. To paraphrase Henry David Thoreau, Go confidently in the direction of your dream. Live the life you have always imagined.

Exhibit your truth proudly. Tell your story. Embrace what matters most to you. Claim your unique place in the world.

Have fun. Be more.

ACKNOWLEDGMENTS

Sitting in a non-descript campus coffee shop for our first real discussion of this book, we were blissfully ignorant of all that we didn't know. Along the way, we've learned a lot, a lot about writing, about self-publishing, and about fitting the work around our full-time jobs. And we learned that the people around us have been more supportive and more helpful than we could ever have dreamed. The evolution of *Be More*, and particularly the SVP Exercise, from an idea developed over the course of many years and countless conversations with friends and colleagues into this book required the work of an amazing team of individuals.

From the first outline forward, no one touched the book more than Eve Stout at Bolthouse Farms. Through countless revisions, the complicated work of both writing the book and then self-publishing, scheduling phone calls and meetings, balancing all of the work at Bolthouse Farms with this project, and generally keeping everyone on the same page, she was indispensable. We are so appreciative of her efforts.

Throughout the process, both the Campbell Soup Company and Bolthouse Farms have been enormously supportive. We are humbled by the willingness of Campbell's President and CEO, Denise Morrison, to participate in the project, adding very relevant and important insights. At Campbell's, Anthony Sanzio, Beth Jolly, Ellen Kagan, Faith Greenfield, and Jill Johnston were early readers and advocates.

Through the years, Jeff Dunn has been a steadfast mentor, consistently encouraging this endeavor and embodying the concept of being true to yourself and getting what you want out of life. This book would not have happened without his incredible push to be mission-driven, strategy-led, and culture-inspired.

We deeply appreciate the decision by Sam Kass to add his story in the foreword in support of *Be More* and its mission of helping people get more out of life.

A group of close friends have served as sounding boards and confidantes, reading multiple versions of the book and providing resources and support at every turn. Doug Worple, Shawn Parr, Cathleen Walters, and Karen McCullough all have shaped *Be More* in very tangible and significant ways. Their comments helped improve the flow of the book and added meaningful perspectives to the story of how the SVP Exercise can bring a greater measure of fulfillment, whether that means a life-changing job search or embracing the opportunities offered in a current job situation.

In particular, the early advice from Rusty Rueff to go "one click down" encouraged us to push harder and to add a depth to the book that was truly transformative. Even more, Rusty's advice about publishing, his encouragement, and his always smart insights were indispensable and so appreciated.

Other readers, too, offered insights that allowed us to enhance the book in ways that made it more relatable and more authentic. Thanks to Tim Owen, Eric Weber, Bill Levisay, Garet Turner, Gretchen Hitze, Ryan Schick, Paul Zimmerman, Sue Robinson, and Connie Swain for your input.

We had worked on the book for several months when in the same moment, we realized that interviewing individuals about working through SVP, whether recently or as it was being developed, would enhance the narrative. The insights and experiences shared by Jeff Crow, Peter Kaye, Eric Johnson, Julie Soley, and others added texture and humanity to the book.

There are only so many times you can read your own work and still see the words on the page in front of you. Thanks to Leonard Nash for a thoughtful content edit that clarified and solidified our final text. Brian

Leung, thank you for helping us find our way to Leonard. Thanks as well to Jon See for the line edits that gave us the confidence to know we were ready to share the book with others.

The decision to self-publish *Be More* was a lot about control: Control of content, control of look, control of schedule. Self-publishing meant self-determination. It also meant an enormous amount of work. Thanks to the incredible production team who got us from a simple Word document to finished book. On the printing side, thanks to the always reliable Susan Casalini; it was a pleasure to work with you again.

From that first conversation in the coffee shop, graphics were always going to be an important part of telling this story. Designer April Bobeck did a terrific job of bringing that vision to life. Our web master Bobby Dorn created the electronic platform that allowed us to begin sharing our message in the months before the book was published. That they, too, are Boilermakers makes us smile.

Additional support on the Bolthouse Farms side came from Pam Naumes for her thoughts on our social media approach to promotion and Brenda Spivak, who responded to our design questions. At Purdue, Kristy Foster, Kristen Hunt, Chris Sharp, Catherine LaBelle, and Abbey Kochert provided endless support and encouragement. Special thanks to Elena Sparger for compiling the book's Notes, a task we were happy to leave in your hands.

Throughout the entire process, our families were gracious and supportive in their willingness to forgo time with us to accommodate many, many book calls and hundreds of emails. Thank you, Rachel, Bailey, and Noah, and Gary, Ted, and Elena for your patience.

TODD PUTMAN *&* LORI SPARGER

AUTHOR'S NOTE

A camp counselor at Camp Carson said to me one night, "Always have a flashlight, it will make it easier to get home." I'm not exactly sure why he said "home" versus "back to your bunk post that midnight pee run," but of course I stayed up that night and over analyzed the idea of always having a bright flashlight to get places. I was so meta at ten.

Now that metaphor has turned into always pushing to surround myself with the right team for the job at hand. People who can guide me places I want to go. I'm not great at a lot of things, but choosing people for a particular journey is a strong suit. And choosing Lori Sparger to help me get *Be More* out of my head and onto paper was a "scathingly brilliant" choice. Her ability to translate my voice, my mumbles, and sometimes even just facial gestures was incredible. We wouldn't be here without her commitment, passion, and capability.

Thank you, Lori. Thanks for lighting the way home!

THE AUTHORS

TODD PUTMAN

A consumer strategist at heart and advocate for mission-driven organizations and individuals that create value while delivering societal benefit, Todd Putman serves as General Manager for the Garden Fresh strategic business unit within the new Campbell Fresh division of the Campbell Soup Company. Todd leads the retail fresh soup business and the recently-acquired Garden Fresh Gourmet. The #1 branded refrigerated salsa in the United States, the Garden Fresh Gourmet acquisition represents the reshaping of Campbell's portfolio toward the fast-growing packaged fresh and organic food categories.

Previously, Todd was the Chief Commercial Officer of Bolthouse Farms, where his duties included sales, consumer and customer marketing, innovation, and research & development.

The mission at Bolthouse Farms is to Inspire the Fresh Revolution, and Todd has dedicated himself to doing just that. He recently served as an architect of "TeamFNV," a brand collaboration focused on increasing consumption and sales of fruits and vegetables among teens and moms. Previously, he was deeply involved in "Eat Brighter," created to encourage children to make the choice to eat more fruits and vegetables. Both partnerships included the White House and First Lady Michelle Obama's *Let's Move!* Initiative and the Produce Marketing Association, among others.

Prior to joining Bolthouse, Todd was President and Managing Director of The Future Pull Group, an innovation and marketing consultancy firm that advises purpose-built brands, particularly those competing in the health/wellness and retail sectors. He has over 30 years of experience in general management, marketing, and innovation with powerhouse brands like Procter & Gamble, The Walt Disney Company, and The Coca-Cola Company.

Todd earned a bachelor's degree from Purdue University, and now chairs the College of Liberal Arts Dean's Advisory Council. His other board affiliations include The Public Good Projects in New York. He was formerly on the board of Sahale Snacks, which was acquired by the J.M. Smucker's Company. Todd is passionately committed to empowering people to accomplish their goals and realize their individual potential. He lives in Los Angeles with his wife, Rachel, and two children.

LORI SPARGER

A proven non-profit, arts, and higher education leader, Lori Sparger is Chief Operating Officer for the College of Liberal Arts at Purdue University. A member of the Dean's leadership team, she collaborates on setting strategic direction and implementing policies and initiatives to advance the mission of the College. She also serves as the College's chief innovation officer, working with the Dean on new initiatives and program development.

Previously, she was Director of Advancement for Purdue's College of Liberal Arts and with her team consistently surpassed annual goals and raised the bar for private support of the College during her six years in the role.

Lori orchestrated an alumni volunteer-led effort that developed the College's new tagline, "Think Broadly. Lead Boldly." Elements of the strategic messaging project are now being incorporated into the College's narrative, which envisions the Liberal Arts in the 21st century as a force for good in the world.

All of her more than 17 years at Purdue have been spent in the College because of her personal passion for the timeless, relevant, and essential importance of the Liberal Arts in higher education and broadly for the benefit of society. She previously served as the College's Director of Development and as Director of Marketing and Donor Relations for Purdue Theatre. Before that, she was Director of Publications at Wabash College and a journalist for a suburban Indianapolis newspaper chain.

Lori received her bachelor's degree in English from Purdue. She serves on the West Lafayette Public Art Selection Group and the Florence H. Lonsford Fund for art acquisitions at Purdue. One of her great pleasures is helping people recognize their gifts and step into themselves. As a writer, she is committed to telling stories that matter. She resides in West Lafayette with her husband, Gary, and two children.

NOTES

INTRODUCTION

1. Brownstone, Sydney. "The Kids Are Alright: Millennials Want Meaningful Jobs That Fix Social Problems." Fast Coexist. Fast Company & Inc., 18 Jul. 2013. Web. http://www.fastcoexist.com/1682573/the-kids-are-alright-millennials-want-meaningful-jobs-that-fix-social-problems

2. Curtis, Lisa. "The Millennial Dilemma: Just A Job Or Truly Meaningful Work?" Elevate. Forbes.com, 2 May 2012. Web. http://www.forbes.com/sites/85broads/2012/05/02/the-millennial-dilemma-just-a-job-or-truly-meaningful-work/

3. Falk, Tyler. "Millennials want jobs that are meaningful to society." ZDNet. CBS Interactive, 18 Jul. 2013. Web. http://www.smartplanet.com/blog/bulletin/millennials-want-jobs-that-are-meaningful-to-society/

4. Licina, Sanja. "How has the Recession Shaped Career Attitudes of Millennials?" The Hiring Site. Careerbuilder, 19 Apr. 2011. Web. http://thehiringsite.careerbuilder.com/2011/04/19/how-has-the-recession-shaped-career-attitudes-of-millennials/

   and Lisa Johnson Mandell., *Millennials are Looking for Meaningful Work*. WN, 25 March 2011. Web. http://wn.com/millennials_are_looking_for_meaningful_work

5. Liu, Betty. "Why Jeffrey Katzenberg Thinks You Should Stop Following Your Passion." LinkedIn Pulse. 4 May 2014. Web. https://www.linkedin.com/today/post/article/20140504142838-123941699-there-s-no-i-in-team-but-there-is-an-e-for-entrepreneur?trk=object-title

6. Reaney, Patricia. "Dream job? Most U.S. workers want to change careers - poll." Reuters. Thomson Reuters, 1 Jul. 2013. Web. http://mobile.reuters.com/article/idUSBRE96015Z20130701?irpc=932

7. Salzberg, Barry. "What Millennials Want Most: A Career That Actually Matters." Forbes Leadership Forum. Forbes.com LLC, 3 Jul. 2012. Web. http://www.forbes.com/sites/forbesleadershipforum/2012/07/03/what-millennials-want-most-a-career-that-actually-matters/

8. Various Authors. "The Happiness Factor." *Harvard Business Review*. Harvard Business Publishing, Jan.-Feb. 2012. Web. http://lifebeyondgrowth.wordpress. com/2012/03/28/harvard-business-review-jan-2012-issue-on-the-happiness-factor/

CHAPTER 1 – PROJECT YOU

1. Esfahani Smith, Emily and Jennifer L. Aaker. "Millennial Searchers." The New York Times. The New York Times Company, 20 Nov. 2013. Web. http://www.nytimes.com/2013/12/01/opinion/sunday/millennial-searchers. html?pagewanted=1&_r=3&hp&rref=opinion&

2. Fitzgerald, F. Scott. *The Great Gatsby*. Scribner. New York. 2004. page 48. Print.

3. Schneider, Peter, master class, Purdue Theatre.

4. Schwartz, Ariel. "Millennials Want Companies That Work On Innovative Ways To Fix The World." Fast Coexist. Fast Company & Inc., 7 Feb. 2014. Web. http:// www.fastcoexist.com/3025989/millennials-want-companies-that-work-on-innovative-ways-to-fix-the-world?partner=rss&utm_source=feedburner&utm_ medium=feed&utm_campaign=feedburner+fastcoexist&utm_content=feedburner

CHAPTER 2 – HAVE WE LOST OURSELVES?

1. Achler, Mark. "GS300 L.A. Influentials presentation." Purdue Liberal Arts, 30 Sept. 2013.

2. Einstein, Albert as quoted by QuoteInvestigator. Web. http://quoteinvestigator. com/2013/01/01/einstein-imagination/

3. Eler, Alicia. "Study: Why Do People Use Facebook?" readwrite. Wearable World Inc., 16 Jan. 2012. Web. http://readwrite.com/2012/01/16/study_why_do_people_ use_facebook

4. Feltman, Rachel. "Most men would rather shock themselves than be alone with their thoughts." The Washington Post. The Washington Post, 3 July 2014. Web. http://www.washingtonpost.com/news/to-your-health/wp/2014/07/03/ most-men-would-rather-shock-themselves-than-be-alone-with-their-thoughts/?Post+generic=?tid%3Dsm_twitter_washingtonpost

5. Green, Maxine. Edutopia.org.

6. "The Oxford Dictionaries Word of the Year 2013 is…." OxfordWords blog. Oxford University Press, 18 Nov. 2013. Web. http://blog.oxforddictionaries.com/2013/11/ word-of-the-year-2013-winner/

7. Rowe, Margaret as quoted by Kayla Gregory in "What's in a Name?" *Liberal Arts Magazine*. Purdue University Press, Fall 2006. Web. http://www.cla.purdue.edu/ news/magazine/documents/2006Fall.pdf

8. University of Virginia. "Doing something is better than doing nothing for most people, study shows." EurekAlert! American Association for the Advancement of Science, 3 July 2014. Web. http://www.eurekalert.org/pub_releases/2014-07/uov-dsio63014.php

CHAPTER 3 – NOBODY CARES

William Shakespeare. "Act I, scene vii." *Macbeth.* , Act I, scene vii

CHAPTER 4 – GOALS

1. Mueller, Pam A. et al. "The Pen Is Mightier Than the Keyboard: Advantages of Longhand Over Laptop Notetaking." *Psychological Science*, 4 June 2014. Web. http://pss.sagepub.com/content/25/6/1159

2. Rueff, Rusty as quoted by Quentin Fottrell in "A shorter workweek may make you a better worker." MarketWatch. MarketWatch Inc., 22 Jul. 2014. Web. http://www.marketwatch.com/story/a-shorter-workweek-may-make-you-a-better-worker-2014-07-22?siteid=rss&rss=1

3. Jobs, Steve as quoted by GoodReads. Web. http://www.goodreads.com/quotes/463176-you-can-t-connect-the-dots-looking-forward-you-can-only

4. Street, Picabo as quoted by GoodReads. Web. http://www.goodreads.com/work/quotes/1489523-picabo-nothing-to-hide

CHAPTER 5 – SKILLS

CHAPTER 6 – VALUES

1. Davila, Joanne et al. "Frequency and quality of social networking among young adults: Associations with depressive symptoms, rumination, and corumination." *Psychology of Popular Media Culture*. American Psychological Association, Apr 2012. p. 72-86. Web. http://psycnet.apa.org/?&fa=main.doiLanding&doi=10.1037/a0027512

CHAPTER 7 – PASSION

1. Docspy. "Passion definition." *Urban Dictionary*. 17 Jan. 2006. Web. http://www.urbandictionary.com/define.php?term=Passion

2. Froh, Jeffrey J. , and Todd B. Kashdan, Charles Yurkewicz, Jinyan Fan, Jennifer Allen, Jessica Glowacki. "The benefits of passion and absorption in activities: Engaged living in adolescents and its role in psychological well-being," *The Journal of Positive Psychology*. Routledge, 4 August 2010. p. 311 – 332. http://www.people.hofstra.edu/Jeffrey_J_Froh/spring%202010%20web/ELYS_FINAL%20PROOF.pdf

3. Jensen, Joli. "Struggling to Find a Project That Excites You? Follow the Lilt." Vitae. The Chronicle of Higher Education, 13 May 2014. Web. https://chroniclevitae.com/news/493-struggling-to-find-a-project-that-excites-you-follow-the-lilt?cid=at&utm_source=at&utm_medium=en

4. Walton, Sam as quoted by qotd.org. Web. http://www.qotd.org/search/search.html?aid=6135

CHAPTER 8 – REALITY CHECK

1. Fitzgerald, F. Scott as quoted by What You Looking At in "Fitzgerald." Poejazzi, 5 Feb. 2013. Web. http://www.poejazzi.com/fitzgerald/

2. Loren, Sophia as quoted by Goodreads. Web. http://www.goodreads.com/quotes/8746-there-is-a-fountain-of-youth-it-is-your-mind

3. Obama, Barack as quoted by Goodreads. Web. http://www.goodreads.com/quotes/170791-making-your-mark-on-the-world-is-hard-if-it

   "Our Past, Our Future & Vision for America." Campus Progress Annual Conference. 12 Jul. 2006. Web. http://obamaspeeches.com/082-Campus-Progress-Annual-Conference-Obama-Speech.htm

4. "What is the Butterfly Effect?" wiseGEEK. Conjecture Corporation, 2003-2015. Web. http://www.wisegeek.org/what-is-the-butterfly-effect.htm

CHAPTER 9 – ADDING IT UP

1. Clandfield, Lindsay. "Writing skills: Mini saga." One Stop English. MacMillan Publishers Ltd., 2000-2015. Web. http://www.onestopenglish.com/skills/writing/lesson-plans/writing-skills-mini-saga/146335.article

2. Drucker, Peter F. as quoted by Goodreads. Web. http://www.goodreads.com/author/quotes/12008.Peter_F_Drucker

3. Wooden, John as quoted by BrainyQuote. Web. http://www.brainyquote.com/quotes/quotes/j/johnwooden446997.html

CHAPTER 10 – APPLYING SVP

1. Amos, Lalita. "GS300 L.A. Influentials presentation." Purdue Liberal Arts. 30 Aug. 2013.

CHAPTER 11 – EVERYTHING CHANGES

1.   Jobs, Steve. Stanford University Commencement 2005.

CHAPTER 12 – WHAT'S NEXT?

1.   Mandela, Nelson as quoted by BrainyQuote. Web. http://www.brainyquote.com/quotes/quotes/n/nelsonmand391070.html

CPSIA information can be obtained
at www.ICGtesting.com
Printed in the USA
LVHW070312100122
708164LV00008B/155